# CAMBRIDGE LIBRARY COLLECTION

*Books of enduring scholarly value*


## Archaeology

The discovery of material remains from the recent or the ancient past has always been a source of fascination, but the development of archaeology as an academic discipline which interpreted such finds is relatively recent. It was the work of Winckelmann at Pompeii in the 1760s which first revealed the potential of systematic excavation to scholars and the wider public. Pioneering figures of the nineteenth century such as Schliemann, Layard and Petrie transformed archaeology from a search for ancient artifacts, by means as crude as using gunpowder to break into a tomb, to a science which drew from a wide range of disciplines - ancient languages and literature, geology, chemistry, social history - to increase our understanding of human life and society in the remote past.

## Devia Cypria

The archaeologist D. G. Hogarth (1862–1927) excavated in Cyprus, Egypt, Greece and Asia Minor over the course of his career. He wrote books about his excavations and travels to bring archaeology to a popular audience. His *A Wandering Scholar in the Levant* (1896; also reissued in this series) was described by T. E. Lawrence as 'one of the best travel books ever written'. Hogarth later became president of the Royal Geographical Society, and Keeper of the Ashmolean Museum, Oxford, from 1908 to 1927. This work, first published in 1889, describes his travels around Cyprus in the summer following his excavations at Old Paphos. He visited areas that had not been examined by archaeologists before, and the book contains many illustrations of buildings and objects he found during his journey, providing details of sites and landscapes still of interest to those studying the history of the island or of archaeology.

Cambridge University Press has long been a pioneer in the reissuing of out-of-print titles from its own backlist, producing digital reprints of books that are still sought after by scholars and students but could not be reprinted economically using traditional technology. The Cambridge Library Collection extends this activity to a wider range of books which are still of importance to researchers and professionals, either for the source material they contain, or as landmarks in the history of their academic discipline.

Drawing from the world-renowned collections in the Cambridge University Library, and guided by the advice of experts in each subject area, Cambridge University Press is using state-of-the-art scanning machines in its own Printing House to capture the content of each book selected for inclusion. The files are processed to give a consistently clear, crisp image, and the books finished to the high quality standard for which the Press is recognised around the world. The latest print-on-demand technology ensures that the books will remain available indefinitely, and that orders for single or multiple copies can quickly be supplied.

The Cambridge Library Collection brings back to life books of enduring scholarly value (including out-of-copyright works originally issued by other publishers) across a wide range of disciplines in the humanities and social sciences and in science and technology.

# Devia Cypria

*Notes of an Archaeological Journey in Cyprus in 1888*

D. G. Hogarth

CAMBRIDGE UNIVERSITY PRESS

Cambridge, New York, Melbourne, Madrid, Cape Town,
Singapore, São Paolo, Delhi, Tokyo, Mexico City

Published in the United States of America by Cambridge University Press, New York

www.cambridge.org
Information on this title: www.cambridge.org/9781108041935



This edition first published 1889
This digitally printed version 2012

ISBN 978-1-108-04193-5 Paperback

# DEVIA CYPRIA

*HOGARTH*

Oxford
HORACE HART, PRINTER TO THE UNIVERSITY

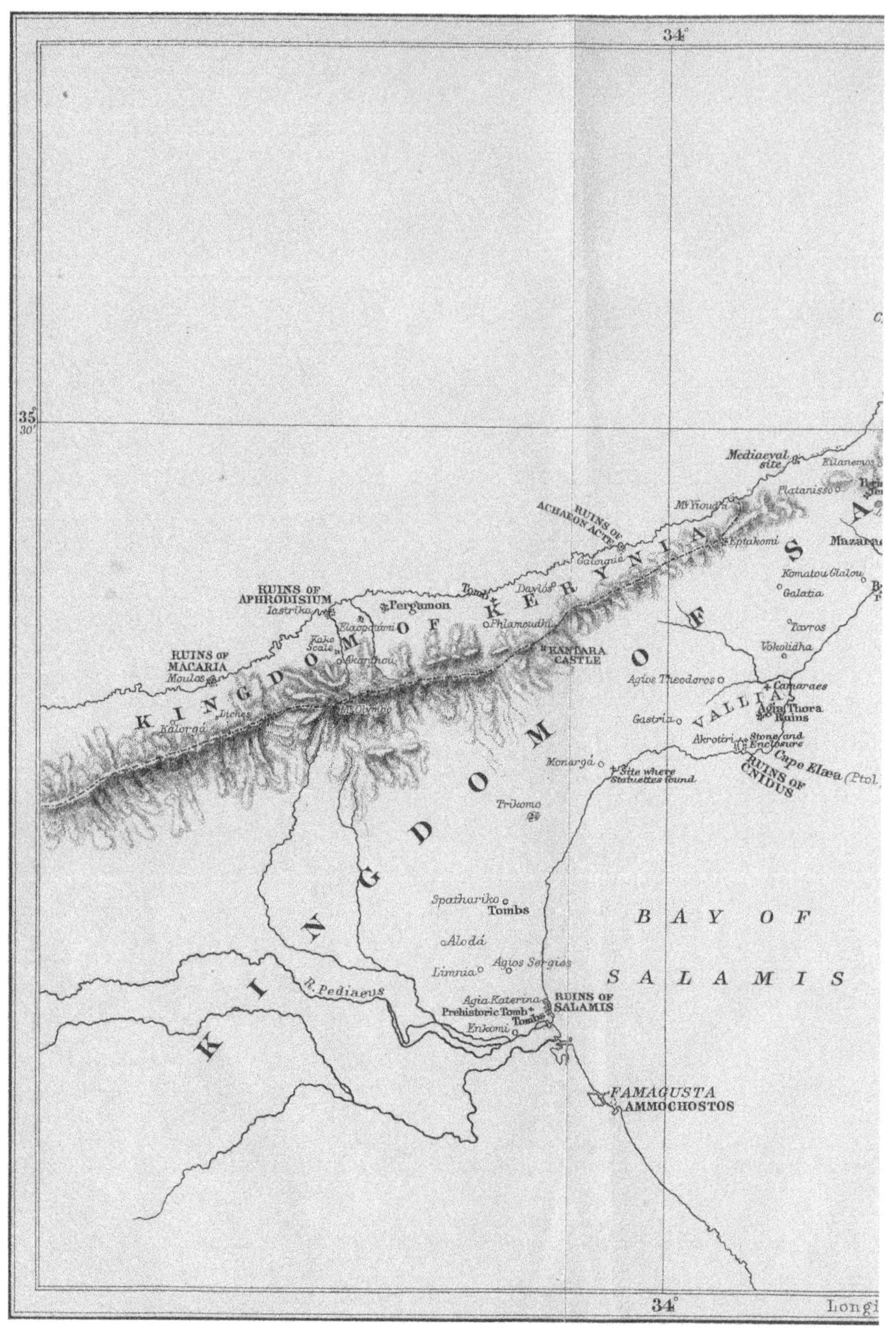

34°
35°
30′
Mediaeval site
Kilanemos
Platanisso
Mt Yiouda
RUINS OF ACHAEON ACTE
Eptakomi
Mazara
Galounia
Komatou Glalou
Galatia
RUINS OF APHRODISIUM
Iastrika
Pergamon
Tomb
Davlos
Elaopatomi
Phlamoudhi
Tavros
Kako Scale
Akanthou
KANTARA CASTLE
Vokolidha
RUINS OF MACARIA
Moulos
Agios Theodoros
Camaraes
Agia Thora
Ruins
Gastria
VALLIA
Liches
Kalorga
Akrotiri
Stone and Enclosure
Cape Elæa (Ptol
RUINS OF CNIDUS
Monarga
Site where Statuettes found
KINGDOM OF KERYNIA
KINGDOM OF SA
KINGDOM
Trikomo
Spathariko
Tombs
BAY OF SALAMIS
Aloda
Agios Sergios
Limnia
R. Pediaeus
Agia Katerina
RUINS OF SALAMIS
Prehistoric Tomb
Tombs
Enkomi
FAMAGUSTA
AMMOCHOSTOS
34°
Longi

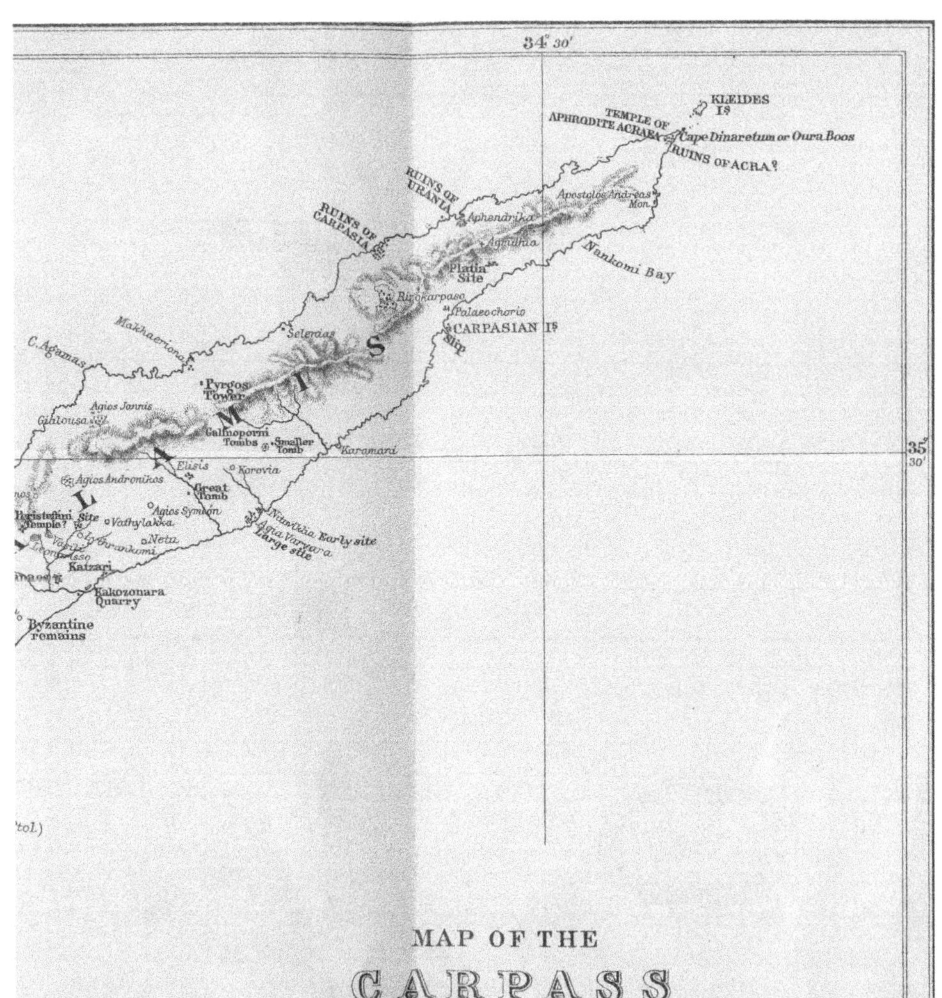


# MAP OF THE
# CARPASS

**Showing the situation of all ancient sites and remains**

*Adapted from the Key Map of the Ordnance Survey.*

Scale. 1 Inch = 5 English Miles

0 1 2 3 4 5 10 15

# DEVIA CYPRIA

*NOTES OF AN*

*ARCHAEOLOGICAL JOURNEY IN CYPRUS*

*IN 1888*

BY

D. G. HOGARTH, M.A.

FELLOW OF MAGDALEN COLLEGE, LATE CRAVEN FELLOW IN THE UNIVERSITY OF OXFORD

*WITH MAP AND ILLUSTRATIONS*

London

HENRY FROWDE, AMEN CORNER, E.C.

1889

# PREFACE.

In December, 1887, while holding a Craven Travelling Fellowship from the University of Oxford, I was commissioned with others by the Committee of the newly-formed Exploration Fund to conduct researches in Cyprus, by excavation and travel. As is now known to those interested in archaeological matters, we pursued the former method for several months at Leontari Vouno, Old Paphos and Amargetti, and results obtained from these several undertakings have been already published. But towards the end of May the heat and near approach of the wheat-harvest made it expedient to defer further excavations until the next autumn or winter, and my companions all left the island to return to Athens or England. We had made however no surface exploration of any considerable part of the island, and, being under no necessity to return to Oxford until October, I embraced the opportunity of carrying out a plan, formed some months previously, of exploring those districts of Cyprus which had been less frequently or less systematically examined by archaeologists,—to wit, the Papho district and the Carpass. While there might be much of archaeological interest to be discovered—inscriptions Cypriote or Greek, sites of cities yet unidentified, stone monuments, native traditions—it would certainly be useful to know once for all what there was and was *not* existing in a district so open to Asiatic influences and so little known as (for example) the Carpass; and further, it was well to prospect future fields for the energies of the

Exploration Fund. Five months of superintendence of large bodies of native diggers had enabled me to acquire not only a tolerable knowledge of the vernacular of the island, but also some experience of native habits and customs, some knowledge of the obscure workings of the peasant's mind, of his grievances, his standards of value, and the degree in which consciously or unconsciously he uses speech to conceal his thoughts: while the considerable scale on which we had conducted the Kuklia excavations had given me a certain notoriety in the villages, guaranteed my bona fides, and caused me to encounter a less impenetrable crust of assumed stupidity than sometimes falls to the lot of travellers in the Levant. Between the end of May and the middle of August I explored thoroughly the west and east of Cyprus, and saw in passing something of the central portions, accompanied always by Gregorio Antoniou of Larnaca, who had acted as our foreman at Kuklia, and to whose intimate knowledge of his fellow-islanders (gained both legitimately and illegitimately) and extraordinary intelligence I largely owe my fortune in discovering as much as I did in so well-worked a field as Cyprus. Native hospitality was always extended to me, and the wilder the district and poorer the peasants, the pleasanter is often my recollection. To many a host who will never see this little book I should like to tender hearty thanks; and to those who may perhaps see it, notably to English residents in Papho, Limassol, Larnaca and Nicosia, I cannot offer gratitude commensurate with the kindness which they extended to me.

This volume is intended to be a Report only of such objects of archaeological interest as I saw in the course of the summer months: incidents of travel, and moving accidents by flood and field (if any there were), fill enough books of Levantine travel without any addition being made to their number. The order of relation must be in the main geographical, first in the Papho district, then the Carpass, and finally in a short chapter which gathers up the few odds and ends, worth recording, in the rest of Cyprus. But even with the omission of the topics above mentioned, it remains a mere traveller's journal in substance, if not entirely in form; and as no more than that, as not aiming for one moment to be exhaustive on any branch of Cyprian archaeology, I now offer it to any one interested enough in Cyprus to peruse its pages.

Such being the unpretending character of the book, it would be superfluous to enumerate a long list of authorities to whom I am indebted: I trust that I have used none without acknowledgement, and references to Pococke, Engel, Sakellarios, De la Mas Latrie (greatest of Cyprian chroniclers), Von Hammer, Ross, and many others will often be found. From Prof. A. H. Sayce I derived, if not the first impulse, at least strong encouragement to travel in the Carpass, and to the kindness and liberality of the Committee of the Cyprus Exploration Fund I owe a debt of acknowledgement. Dr. F. H. H. Guillemard and Mr. R. Elsey Smith have allowed me to reproduce photographs taken by them, and the last-named contributes an account of the Aschelia carvings (p. 43).

Lastly, but chiefly, to Prof. W. M. Ramsay, of Aberdeen, who has read the proofs throughout, I must record my indebtedness both for thorough and just criticism which has revealed to me many errors, and for most valuable suggestions, many of which I have noted particularly, but for many others I must tender him only a general, but most grateful, acknowledgement.

The major part of the cost of publication has been defrayed by the Craven University Fund in accordance with a decree of Convocation: without that assistance the book would probably not have appeared, and I must tender my thanks especially to Mr. H. F. Pelham, and also to others who were concerned in obtaining and administering the grant.

D. G. H.

MAGDALEN COLLEGE,
*August 30th*, 1889.

# DEVIA CYPRIA.

## CHAPTER I.

### THE PAPHO DISTRICT.

*The kingdom of Paphos.*

AMONG the independent kingdoms and dynasties into which Cyprus was partitioned from the earliest period until the close of the fourth century before our era, Paphos must have ranked at all times, whether in extent of territory, in wealth or fame, second only to Salamis. Nature has defined it so clearly that we can hardly mistake the boundaries in spite of the absence of written authority: on the north and west lies the sea: upon the east the mass of Troodos, continued in the rugged Forest Range to Cape Poumo, interposes a huge barrier between the west and east of the island, which even under Evagoras the kingdom of Salamis appears not to have passed. At the northern end of this barrier the kingdom of Paphos marched with that of Soli. Lastly upon the south the tremendous cleft, cut by the Kostithes river up to Mount Troodos, bounds the kingdom of Curium, which comprised the broad uplands and deep fertile valleys as far as the Episcopi river.

The kingdom of Paphos was therefore an oblong, about thirty miles from north to south, and twenty from east to west; and with the exception of a strip along the coast from Old to New Paphos, and a triangular tract running inland for four miles from the Bay of Arsinoe, entirely mountainous, ridge after ridge starting up from the depression which runs below the Troodos and Forest ranges, and declining to the sea. Through this mountain mass five rivers have cut channels of tremendous depth, the descent and ascent of whose sides makes travelling in the interior so tedious, that few visitors to this part of the island leave the coast-road.

But the Papho hills are by no means unproductive; and sterile tracts of rock and scrub are to be found indeed in the Akámas or Oridhes, but hardly anywhere else. The billowy ridges are diversified by large cultivated tracts, and countless flocks graze on their sides: in the south-eastern corner of the old kingdom, round the villages of Arsos, Vasa, and Omodhos, lie the best vineyards in Cyprus: the equable temperature of the uplands is more favourable to the mulberry than in any other part of the island; and the rapid fall of the rivers renders easy the irrigation of the valleys. Moreover, Troodos acts as a screen against those northerly and easterly winds which parch the Mesaoréa, and thus arises a common Cypriote saying, that when Papho is full the rest of Cyprus is hungry.

The poverty and barbarism of the modern Paphiti are due therefore not to the niggardliness of the soil, but to isolation from those parts of the island where communication is easy, and whither civilisation and commerce have been attracted since the Middle Ages; but when the port of New Paphos was still one of the very best, if not absolutely the best, in the island (as must have been the case in the days of small craft) the condition of the district to which it affords a ready outlet was probably very different. The great extent of the ruins of New Paphos itself speaks to its former greatness; to the south the richest of Aphrodite's shrines (according to Pausanias) attracted pilgrims from all parts of the Mediterranean; in the north lay Arsinoe, a place of much wealth if we may judge from the character of its lately discovered necropolis; and inland are many relics of better times, contrasting markedly with the poverty-stricken villages of to-day. Letymbou with its dozen churches; Amargetti and Drimu, seats of Apollo; Polemi and Kathikas, whose ancient tombs alone attest the existence of forgotten settlements; Limni, Lyso, and Istingio, where old adits and slag-heaps remind us of the ancient fame of the copper-island; and acres of ruin at Cape Drepano, Agios Konon, and Lipati, prove that the Akámas was not always the uninhabited forest region that it is at present.

*Old Paphos.* So long as this district was ruled by an independent king, its capital was the older Paphos, later distinguished as *Παλαιὰ Πάφος*, or *Παλαίπαφος*, from the city ten miles to the north-west which had originally served as its port. In an uncommercial age, when strength of position was chiefly desired, the Kuklia hill, connected only by a narrow isthmus with the ridge behind, was the more natural site for a royal city and a great shrine; but the distance dividing the site from any good harbour, and its defective water-supply, tended rapidly to diminish its importance as compared with that of New Paphos, when the Cyprian towns were no longer dangerous to one another but united in subjection to the Ptolemies; and still more when all the Levant owned in Rome a common mistress. The history of the earliest capital and of the independent kingdom is indissolubly connected with that of the shrine of the Paphian Aphrodite, whose high priests the kings successively were; and upon this and upon the antiquities of its modern representative, Kuklia, it is unnecessary to touch after the full treatment that they have received in the Journal of Hellenic Studies (vol. ix), more especially in the paper contributed by Mr. M. R. James (p. 175). Sufficient to say here that the foundation of the kingdom is lost in the mists of antiquity, for it appears probable that, even before the Cinyrad dynasty was established (which cannot be much later than the tenth century), an older royal family had existed, that of the Cilician Tamiradae (Tac. Hist. ii. 3: Hesych. s. v. *Ταμιραδαί*). In the seventh century a Paphian king paid tribute to Assyria, and from this period until the extinction of the monarchy by Ptolemy Lagus we have the names of twelve kings, who, with others unknown, carried down the Cinyrad dynasty in unbroken succession: and, even when no longer royal, inscriptions of Paphos show the *Ἀρχὸς τῶν Κινυραδῶν* or *Κινύραρχος* to have been a high dignitary, who discharged the actual duties of the temple under the nominal high priest, the *στρατηγὸς τῆς νήσου*. That the power of these kings extended far inland is proved by the existence of inscriptions of a Nicocles in the Cypriote character at Agia Moni on the Panagia hill close to the skirt of the Forest[1]. After the last Nicocles had hanged himself in his palace, Palaepaphus ceased to be distinguished by anything but the sanctity and wealth of its shrine, of which the *στρατηγοὶ τῆς νήσου* continued, like its old kings, to be nominal high priests[2]. But they seem to have resided ordinarily at Salamis, and Palaepaphus could have been no more than the provincial capital of this end of the island; while even this inferior

[1] Infra, p. 32.

[2] J. H. S., vol. ix, Inscriptions of Paphos, Nos. 2, 11, 12, etc.

position had been yielded to its port before the first century of our era, when St. Paul found the proconsul temporarily established at the latter. But the wealth, magnificence, and dignity of the great shrine of Aphrodite was not thereby impaired, for Cato, on taking over the island for Rome, considered its priesthood the best equivalent for royal power which he could offer to the last Ptolemy; and more than a century later it attracted Titus by its fame and splendour.

*New Paphos.*

But from the Roman period the city of Agapenor, formerly known as Erythra[1], usurped the political headship, and when the district had been converted by the labours of St. Epaphras and his successors, became the seat of the first bishop of Paphos, whose cathedral is perhaps represented by the ruins immediately to the north-west of the church of St. George. Under the Lusignan princes it became in 1196 a Latin throne, and by the Concordia of 1222 the Greek prelate, although recognised, was banished to Arsos in the extreme south-east of the district, retaining however his former title. The territory of Paphos was incorporated in the Domain Royal, and as such granted by Guy in 1193 to Amaury, the ex-constable of Jerusalem: but the town by the sea-shore had already been superseded by a new settlement on the bluffs, not quite a mile inland, which has survived through Venetian and Turkish times to be the present administrative capital of the district. Whether the decay of New Paphos proper was due to the unhealthiness of its marshy site, or to the Arab incursions which began in the reign of Heraclius and culminated in the revenge wreaked on Cyprus by Haroun al Raschid, and which drove Carpasia, Lapethus, Aphrodisium and other towns inland, is uncertain, but it seems to be clear that Ktima was already flourishing when Richard of England landed. The old town still retained some importance, and was adorned by the Franks with churches and public buildings, the remains of which are still to be seen: but it occupied only the eastern half of its former site, as does the village of Baffo at this day.

The allusions of ancient authors to this city will be found in Engel (vol. i. pp. 140–144), Sakellarios (*Κυπριακά*, vol. i. pp. 100–106), and the Dictionary of Classical Geography (sub voce). The frequent uncertainty as to which Paphos is intended makes it impossible to be sure as to the features of the Port

[1] Steph. Byz., s.v. Eustath. in Hom., Il. ii. 499.

Town; Strabo tells us that it had a harbour and *ἱερὰ εὖ κατεσκευασμένα*, and one of the latter was in all probability dedicated to Aphrodite. Tradition points at this day to a mound close to the north-west side of the harbour as the site of such a temple; at a rough estimate its summit measures 200 ft. from north to south by 250 ft. east to west: fragments of about twenty monolithic columns of grey granite, 22 inches in diameter, lie on the surface, protrude from the sides, or are built into fences hard by, and from these native exaggeration has given to the mound the name *Σαράντα Κολόννες*. No other remains lie above the surface, but three holes have been sunk into the mound whereby massive foundations and substructures have been exposed: that on the south reveals a vaulted chamber 12 feet high, the southern wall of which has fallen away: to the east of this a narrow stairway runs down from the surface of the mound to a doorway choked with earth; a massive wall can be traced for some feet further, the returning wall being also visible on the east of the mound. In the centre of the summit a shaft has been sunk into similar substructures of a very massive order, and there is evidently a labyrinth of staircases, vaults, and passages underlying the whole mound and awaiting a persevering explorer. As to the date of some portions at any rate of the Temple of which they formed the basement, indications are afforded by the Roman granite columns, already mentioned, and coarse plaster which may be picked up in quantities; but the existence of blocks with a raised panel in the centre and chisel-draft round the edges, similar to those in the lower courses of the Parthenon basement and in pre-Roman work of the second period at Old Paphos, suggest an earlier date for the original building erected on this mound [1]. If it be really true that this is the site of a temple of Aphrodite, (and its commanding position beside the harbour tends to corroborate such a tradition), it might be worth while to explore it more thoroughly with the help of pick and shovel.

The ruins of the city have been often described, notably by Pococke (vol. i. pp. 225 foll.); by Von Hammer (Topographische Ansichten, pp. 134 foll.); by Engel (loc. cit. chiefly from Von Hammer's account); by Sakellarios (loc. cit.); by M. de la Mas Latrie (L'Île de Chypre, pp. 24, 25); by

[1] This fashion of stone-dressing was, however, in vogue in Roman times also.

General di Cesnola (pp. 222 foll.); and by Prof. A. H. Sayce in a letter to the Academy, March 1888; but nevertheless I venture to record the main features again, as my opportunities of making repeated visits to the site sometimes in the company of residents at Ktima who knew the place thoroughly, sometimes with native companions, enabled me to see a good deal which, hidden away in gardens or courtyards, escapes the passing traveller.

The city wall may be traced, by actual remains or by the rock-beds in which the stones have lain, from point to point round the whole circuit, beginning from the breakwater on which the castle now stands, continued round the sea-shore into the northern bay, and then along the cliff top past the modern light-house for a short distance inland. This gives two sides of the quadrangle, which now turns sharply to the south-west. Indeed soon after passing the lighthouse, the tracks have already become very interesting: for 150 feet every 'step' is clearly defined, the wall having been from six to eight feet broad where the cliff is low, and three feet where it is high. A gutter runs along the seaward side. At regular intervals occur sally-ports,—square shafts sunk through the rock and emerging in the plain below; and traces of a gate are apparent leading to a well still in use. A more interesting gate occurs at the end of these 150 feet of wall; it seems to have been flanked by towers, and a sloping way adapted from a natural spur of the rock leads down into the plain. This approach is eight feet in width and curves northwards; at the lower end are rock-cut steps, which suggest that the sea which is now some 50 yards distant, once washed over the stretch of salt marsh up to the cliffs (whose appearance is certainly waterworn) and that this entrance was a water-gate, the steps at the lower end of the approach being cut for the convenience of boats. But if this is fanciful, then the gate leads to the Tombs with which the plain is honeycombed as far as Palaeocastro.

North of the gate the wall can be easily traced for some 400 feet, when it turns at an acute angle south westward, and presently descends into the low ground and is lost for a while. At the angle the remains of a massive bastion and tower can be seen, and a well, descending for a tremendous distance into darkness, has been sunk in the rock itself so that the tower might still be supplied even if the low parts of the city were in hostile hands. The line of the wall may be picked out at intervals along the eastern side of the town, turning westwards at last on a high bluff which still carries remains of masonry, and running straight down to the Harbour a little to the north of the church of St. George where are 'St. Paul's pillars,' and which accordingly stood outside the enceinte. On this side the ground is low, and the remains of a portion of the wall, which exist in a field near the port, show it to have been of great thickness (from 12 to 15 feet), and constructed of a core of cemented rubble, faced with squared stone.

Within the city the most interesting remains are those of the northern breakwater formed like the wall of a rough cemented core, and faced with massive blocks clamped together with metal. This is probably of early origin, for the existence of such a work must have been essential at all times to the security of the harbour: at its base stands a castle which appears to be of Turkish construction. The harbour itself is spacious and sheltered, and much frequented by small craft at this day: it is however only shallow, and, being bottomed with solid rock, cannot readily be improved. Two hundred yards to the north has been hollowed out in the earth a very small amphitheatre, whose arena is not more than 250 feet in circumference: no trace of its stone or marble seating is visible. The same is true of a small theatre in the hill-side, south of the lighthouse, and not far north of the *Σαράντα Κολόννες*. In this portion of the site the lines of two streets are clearly defined, one leading from the Amphitheatre and the other from the Harbour, and converging at a circular ruin, perhaps that of a fountain, where a marble Cupid of Graeco-Roman workmanship was found a few years ago.

This northern half of the site is not now built over, but presents a hillocky waste of stone squared and unsquared, granite shafts, fragments of marble mosaic and concrete, and miscellaneous débris of a late period. The southern half is covered by modern buildings and enclosures, out of which rise the ruins of a large building, probably a church, of the Lusignan epoch on the north of the new road, and in the vaults under this structure a number of stone escutcheons have been found, certain of which are now built into a bath at Ktima. Another church, apparently Latin, stands a hundred yards further south, and close to the city wall west of this two plain granite shafts, apparently in situ, project from the soil about 20 feet apart, and an immense number of similar columns are built into walls or peep out of the ground in this neighbourhood. A mediaeval stone lion lies on the top of a fence hard by.

Immediately without the wall lie the foundations of the early Greek cathedral (?) already mentioned, and under the church of Agios Giorgios, must be the remains of the temple of which four massive granite shafts stand in situ, deeply buried in the soft earth which covers the whole site; General di Cesnola has made some attempt to clear the bases of those two with which St. Paul's name is connected by tradition, the apostle being reputed to have been tied to the northernmost and flogged, and to have left, some twelve feet up, the mark of his blood (which runs red on St. *John's* day!). The south-eastern angle of the peribolus wall of this temple is seen under the fences of the modern enclosure. A second temple seems to have stood where the easternmost church on the site, Agios Antonios, now lies in ruins: and about the tiny churches of Agia Marina and Phaneromene to the north, and indeed over all the space between that and Agios Giorgios, is a network of massive foundations, showing that a large suburb existed outside the wall on this side. The tombs are for the most part on the north and east of the city, only two isolated groups, remarkable for their Cypriote inscriptions, being found about a quarter of a mile to the south. These have been described in the article 'Tombs' in the Journal of Hellenic Studies, vol. ix. pp. 267 foll., and the more remarkable of the tombs at Palaeocastro by General di Cesnola (p. 223) and others. The bluffs of Ktima are also full of graves, pertaining to New Paphos, but so thorough has been the search for treasure in past ages that it would be probably impossible to find a single unrifled tomb, nor has any tradition of the character of the spoil survived. The following inscriptions, not previously published, I found at one time or another on this site.

1. Pedestal of grey limestone in four fragments, now in Hadji Ianniko's garden, broken top and a good deal chipped: a considerable piece gone on the left.

ΩΙυΥΕΙΛΙΩΙΜΑΙUΙΙΩΙΙΩ//////ΔΕΛΦ/////
ΟΥΟΥΕΙΛΙΟΥΤΟΥΞΤΡΑΤΗΓⱵ/////ΑΝΤΟΣ
ΣΕΠΑΡΧΕΙΑΣΚΑΙΛΕΥΚΙΟΥΟΥΕ//·///·//·//ΟΥ
ΠΑΤΟΥΤ/ΩΙΠΑΤΡΩΝΙΤΟΚΟΙΝΟΝΤΟ//·//ΥΠΡΙΩΝ

*Γαί]ῳ (?) Οὐειλίῳ Μα(ρον)ίῳ(?) τῷ [ἀ]δελφ[ῷ*
*. . . Οὐειλίου τοῦ στρατηγή[σ]αντος*
*τῆς Κυπρία]ς ἐπαρχείας καὶ Λευκίου Οὐε[ιλί]ου*
*τοῦ ἀνθυ]πάτου τῷ πατρῶνι τὸ κοινὸν τὸ [Κ]υπρίων.*

This inscription adds another to the meagre list of Roman governors of Cyprus [1].

The cognomina of the three brothers being identical, the lapicide has not repeated them. It is certainly curious to find the legatus pro praetore placed before the proconsul. The third brother had probably represented the island at Rome in some matter, while his brothers were in command in Cyprus itself—a curious instance of the farming of a province among a family.

2. Cut in large letters on a split column of grey limestone in the same garden.

ΠΑΦΟΥ *Πάφου.*

3. On a fragment of white marble lying not far from the church of St. George.

Q . DES : AIT : L'AME.

4. On a split column of white marble found in the same neighbourhood.

+ ICI GIST : HARIOR (?)
BEDOUIN : E SON PE-
RE : S : P . DE BEDOUIN
QUE : DIEUS : AIT L
ARME :

5. To these inscriptions may be added a scarabaeus shown to me in Ktima by M. Cleoboulos, assessor of the District Court. It is said to have been found near Chrysochou, and is beautifully engraved with a group of Heracles, armed with bow, quiver, and skin, wrestling with a lion, while behind him stands a draped female figure, without any distinguishing attributes. Over the group are cut the following characters:—

[1] See the end of this volume for an enumeration of all the pro-consular governors whose names are known to me. The list is as complete as I can make it, but the sources of evidence are so scattered that I cannot be sure of having exhausted all possibilities.

i. e. *Διϝειθέμιϝος*, genitive of the name *Διϝείθεμις* which occurs in the twenty-first line of the bronze tablet of Dali (Sammlung der griech. dialekt-Inschr. i. p. 28). I was unable to take an impression of the scarab, or to examine it satisfactorily; but I should judge the lettering to be of the fourth century B. C.

*The Akámas.* Between New Paphos and Cape Drepano lies a fertile strip of coastland, abounding in villages, and destitute only of antiquities; but at a line drawn from the latter cape to the mouth of the Poli river begins the wild forest-tract of the Akámas, so-called from the ancient name of its extreme northern point, which, except for two or three villages on the summit and east of the central ridge and hardly to be included in the district at all, is devoid of human habitation other than isolated tchifliks or huts inhabited only in summer. It is a sterile corner of Cyprus, thickly covered with scrub, abounding in deep gullies and bold rock formations, the central spine being broken into bold peaks or miniature table mountains; here and there in a tiny valley is a cultivated patch, but nine-tenths of the district produces nothing but game.

Its ancient remains proved less interesting than I had been led to expect, but they sufficiently prove that the district was once much more thickly inhabited than now. The headland of Drepano is covered with the ruins of a Roman town; no village exists very near to it, and the structures seem to have been thrown down by only natural agencies; the walls range from 1 to 2½ feet thick, but so far as can be seen among the piles of grey stone and the dense forest of 'schinia,' the buildings were quite small—mostly dwelling-houses. In the centre of the low ridge, on the top and south of which the town was situated, are remains of a small amphitheatre, and near it massive ruins of a large church. Fragments of cornice are frequent, but nothing on the site speaks of great antiquity; and the plain marble shafts which stand at the west end of the little church of St. George, as well as the marble Byzantine altar (shaped like an hour-glass), are quite late. In the top of the cliff to the north have been cut several cisterns, and in the seaward face two remarkable tiers of graves, one above the other, the dividing floor being so thin that in several places it has either given way of itself, or been easily broken through by *τυμβωρύχοι*. The upper tier contains large tombs with shallow arched *μνήματα* or sepulchral niches, each with a rock-bed, and lying *parallel* to the side of the tomb itself. The tombs of the lower tier however have *μνήματα* which radiate at right angles to the central hall, and as the latter arrangement appears (see the article 'Tombs' in J. H. S. p. 265) to be the older in Cyprus, we may perhaps conclude that the two tiers are of different periods. In a large tomb of the lower series measuring 17 feet 8 inches × 9 feet I found two names cut over *μνήματα*, one

6. ΒΙΚΑΡΙΟΥ *Βικαρίου*

merely scratched, the other,

7. ΦΙΛΑΙΟΥ *Φιλαίου*

ΝΙΚΙΟ *Νικίο(υ)*,

very deeply incised in letters six inches long. Other tombs are scored with crosses showing that they had been sanctified a second time for Christian uses.

Nearly a mile inland at a spot known as Meleti is another group of ten tombs, arranged like the spokes of a wheel in an isolated mass of rock, and all rifled long ago. Their chief characteristics are spaciousness and abundance of rock-cut mouldings: the doors have *πρόθυρα* sometimes flanked with pilasters, and approached by from eight to fifteen steps, and the *μνήματα* are few and elaborately ornamented, one having a triple portico supported on square pilasters, giving access to a recess containing the sepulchral bed. Over the centre

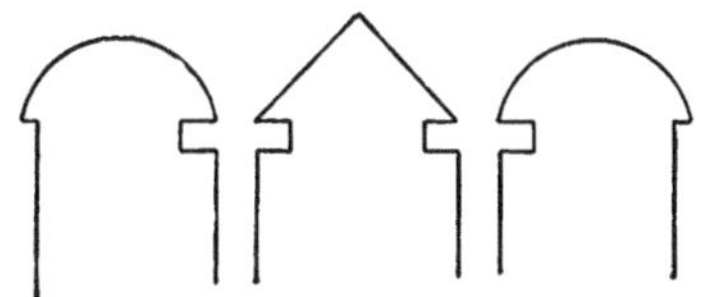

of this portico is a deep incision in the rock suggesting that an inscription has been abstracted, as by Count de Vogüé from the *Σπήλαιον τῆς 'Ρηγινῆς* at Kuklia. But I can find no record of the finding here of any such text, Cypriote or Greek, and the only inscription now to be seen in any of the group is ΚΑΙϹΥ (*καὶ σύ*) cut over a *μνῆμα*: a number of crosses prove that, whoever originally made these graves, they were certainly used at some period by Christians.

Off the extremity of Drepano lies the island of St. George, on which the Commissioner, Captain Thompson, assured me that there were cisterns similar to those on the mainland; between the cape and the island runs a reef which may have contributed to form a small natural harbour. To the ancient name of this town there exists no kind of clue: Strabo only mentions the Ἀκάμας between Paphos and Arsinoe; Ptolemy names Δρέπανον ἄκρον but says nothing of a city. If there were any ground whatever for asserting, as does Sakellarios (vol. i. p. 109), that the Cyprian Alexandria, mentioned by Eustathius, Stephen of Byzantium, and the Chronicon Pascale[1], was situated κατὰ ταῦτα τὰ μέρη, these might be its ruins, being the most considerable of this district yet unidentified; but the name Capo de Alessandretta found in a Venetian map by D'Anville, and in the Isolario of Porcacchi is attached to a point of the coast beyond Poli-tis-Chrysochou in which neighbourhood was also the Lusignan cazal of Alexandretta, and we are compelled to give the city on Cape Drepano the choice of any one of the twenty unattached names recorded by Engel (i. pp. 156 foll.)[2].

The account given by General di Cesnola (p. 225) of this site affords a good criterion whereby to judge that gentleman's accuracy or power of observation: he says, 'At this place (i. e. the village of Lemba) a peasant conducted me to the sea-shore through a passage in a craggy ravine to see some rock-cut tombs, which are near a headland called Drepano; but *there are no remains of ancient habitations in the neighbourhood*, though the quantity of tombs there must have belonged to some ancient town not far off. A few hundred yards east of these tombs are the crumbling walls of an early Greek church.' If the General ever went to Drepano at all, how on earth did he miss this mass of ruins, a quarter of a mile square, and situated close above the tombs? And why is the church, which is about fifty yards from the tombs in a southerly direction, said to be 'a few hundred yards east'?

[1] See Engel, vol. i. p. 74.

[2] These are (excluding Acra and Cnidus, which I think that I have identified in the Carpass) Acragas, Argos, Asine, Dionia, Elmaeum and Gerandrum (both probably near Soli), Epidarum, Cinyreia, Cremaseia, Cresion, Cyrene, Lacedaemon, Myricae, Panacrum, Sestus, Satrachus, Tegessus, Tyrra, Tharsis and a city 'Cyprus,' the two last being very doubtful. Cf. Sakellarios, p. 107.

North of the cape the hills approach the sea, and the scenery becomes more wild; the streams cut channels between lofty cliffs, and, forking, leave precipitous masses of rock standing out of their valleys. On such a precipitous plateau, dividing a stream which flows down from Orodhes, are faint traces of an ancient village—a few cippi, squared blocks, plain shafts and caps, and opened tombs being all that remain. The rock is very near the surface, and there is nothing to excavate but a few late graves, and if General di Cesnola ever intended to send workmen here (as one of his former overseers asserted to me) he had been grievously misled. The place is now called Lipati, and lies to the north of the spring of Agios Theodoros; a second spring rises higher up the valley.

From this point to the northern extremity of the peninsula, Cape Arnaüti, stretches unbroken forest; for thirteen miles there is no human habitation except the huts of salt-watchers on Cape Lara and at Gerá-nisos, and shepherds' refuges here and there on the hills, while such tracks as exist are most difficult even for mules to traverse, and jagged gullies must be continually crossed; no road can be found along the sea-shore against which a surf seems to beat even in the calmest weather. But at a point marked on the Survey as Agios Konon and Agios Giorgios, ten miles north of Lipati, are remains of another large village, boasting a perennial holy spring; among the débris are foundations of one of the smallest churches in existence, the whole dimensions being only 14 feet × 7 feet; a much larger church, that called Agios Konon on the map, exists a short distance to the north, and a curious shrine built on to the mouth of a cave, and (to judge from the names cut and scribbled on its frescoes) much frequented by inconsiderate pilgrims, is that called Agios Giorgios[1]. All are mere shells inhabited only by countless myriads of fleas, which swarmed up our persons with exuberant joy after a Lenten abstention probably of many months' duration. The ruins of the village seem to be no older than the churches, and are probably Byzantine. The most noticeable feature is an artificial cave near the largest church, hewn nearly square, a rock pillar being left in the centre to support the roof. As there are no sepulchral niches it seems probable that it was constructed for a dwelling-

[1] Our native guide inverted these dedications, making the southern shrine that of Agios Konon.

place, or to serve the purpose, which it has since fulfilled, of a sheep-fold.

From this point the track crosses the ridge to the Agios Nicóla tchiflik, and we were assured that we could not follow the western coast any farther; but by dint of riding along the beach where there was any, and into the sea, where there was none, we reached the point of Sykarona, the last before Arnaüti itself. Round its base, however, flowed deep water, and we had perforce to turn inland and cross the neck of the cape by ascending a dry gully and descending a precipitous slope; after much difficulty we reached Cape Arnaüti and found the eastern side of the peninsula less rugged than the western, and a fairly level track led down to the shores of the beautiful bay of Poli. Since leaving Agios Konon we had seen no antiquities, and searched in vain near Cape Arnaüti for General di Cesnola's 'ruins of an ancient town between two curiously-shaped conical peaks'; the place indicated must be the deep gap in the central ridge above Agios Minás, on either side of which rise two hills, rather *μαστο-* than *κωνοειδεῖς*, but no trace of any remains exists here, and indeed the only site which shows any vestige of ancient ruins is that on the seashore below the Agios Nicóla tchiflik and opposite to Kakoskalion-nisi which is probably the Stiria Isle of Pliny. Here are the faintest traces of ancient foundations, and a considerable quarry from which stone has probably been cut for transportation to Arsinoe: but General di Cesnola could hardly have intended this, for, though it lies under the (flat-topped) Pyrgo Müti, there is no corresponding hill on the other side.

On this side of the Akámas we enter a land of classical and mediaeval romance; for here, according to Cypriote tradition, was the Fontana Amorosa of Ariosto, and a distinct and far more beautiful *Βρύσις τῶν 'Ερωτῶν*, where the natives say that Aphrodite wedded Acamas. There can be little doubt that the two have probably but one origin, and that the real 'fount of love' is the present *Βρύσις τῶν 'Ερωτῶν*, although the western tradition has identified itself with a separate spring. The latter rises at the foot of the cliff in a tiny bay half-an-hour's ride north of Agios Nicóla, and is a prosaic little fount enough[1]; but the former, three and a half miles to the south, near

[1] The ruins of an old town, mentioned by Engel, i. p. 73, as existing near here, consist only of the remains of a church.

the Potami tchiflik, has no rival in Cyprus. Approaching from the sea the traveller follows a rushing stream up a densely wooded ravine, barred at last by sombre cliffs, whose top can scarcely be discerned through the arch of boughs; spreading and shimmering over the slanting face of the rock falls a mountain stream, until near the base the cliff slopes inwards and the water falls from a forest of maiden-hair fern in a thousand silver threads to the pool below: across the threads here and there shoot stray shafts of sunlight, penetrating the dense shade of a gigantic fig-tree, and three separate springs rise on either side under the cliff and gurgle down to join the pool. The traveller whose eyes have seen only the rock and scrub of waterless Cyprus, seems in an enchanted spot, not seeing from whence the water comes, and he ceases to wonder that native fancy has peopled the spot with legendary loves, and sailors carried westward vague reports of its beauties to the ears of Ariosto[1].

Between the rival fountains and a little back from the coast lies a mediaeval relic now known as Pyrgos, the 'Tower'; an arched gateway gives entrance to a small cloister of which only the northern side is standing, the wall showing traces of fresco. Round about are foundations of out-buildings, and

[1] Orlando Fur. xviii. stanz., 137 foll. Astolpho and his four companions touch at Famagusta on their way from Damascus to France, and, sailing presently round the south of the island, reach Paphos, where they disembark and wander inland :—

Dal mar sei miglia o sette a poco a poco
Si va salendo in verso il colle ameno
Mirti e cedri e naranci e lauri il loco,
E mille altri soavi arbori han pieno—
Serpillo e persa, e rose e gigli, e croco
Spargon dall' odorifero terreno
Tanta soavitá ch' in mar sentire
Lo fa ogni vento che da terra spire.

Da limpida fontana tutta quella
Piaggia rigando va un ruscel secondo
Ben si può dir, che sia di Vener bella
Il luogo dilettevole e giocondo;
Che v' è ogni donna affato, ogni donzella
Piacevol più, ch' altrove sia nel mondo,
E fa la Dea che tutte ardon d' amore
Giovani e vecchie infino all' ultime ore.

'Fontana Amorosa' is a misnomer; the real Fontana Amorosa of Ariosto is the magic spring in the Forest of Arden, twin with the fount of Hate (i. stanz. 76). The Cyprian fount is rather the *Fontana di Venere.*

disused paths lead through the brushwood: east of it is a little spring and some fine pine-trees. There can be no doubt that it was once a small monastery, or a μετοχή of a larger one.

*Interior.* The interior of the kingdom of Paphos is divided into five distinct ridges[1] by the deep valleys of the Poli river, the Ezuza, the Xero, and the Dhiarrizos; and we will describe it in detail beginning with the northernmost division which is bounded by the sea, the mountains, and the Poli river. The remains of Arsinoe which lie at the mouth of the latter have been explored recently by the representatives of the Cyprus Exploration Fund, and their report will render it idle to attempt any description here; we will pass therefore from the Akámas into the interior of the country, which has been (from an archaeological point of view) little known hitherto. As has been already remarked the difficult nature of these hills has deterred most travellers from leaving the main track, which from Arsinoe passes either directly across the western ridge by Critoterra and Orodhes into the Papho plain, or follows the Poli river for a few miles, and crosses by Stroumbi, Polemi, and Tsada to Ktima. Now and then a traveller who, like Pococke, has visited the monastery of Kykko, makes his way by Chrysaorgiatissa and the Ezuza valley to Papho, or coming from Nicosia he may, like St. Barnabas, take the route of the Marathasa valley under Chionistra, and follow the Dhiarrizos

[1] This convenient natural division was for some reason neglected by the Lusignan princes in the partition of the Domain Royal in the Papho district, although the bailiwicks were five in number. For example, in the bailiwick of Chrysochou was Akourdalia, west of the Poli river. That of Emba included Tremithousia in the Chrysochou section, but not Ktima, for the latter pertained to that of Aschelia (l'Échelle of the Hospitallers), which comprised both slopes of the Ezuza valley. The upper part of the Dhiarrizos valley, together with a 'Critu,' which must be Kritou Marottou, fell to Mammonia; while the lower valley, with Lapithiou on the left bank of the Ezuza, and Melia on the right (!) pertained to the bailiwick of Covucho or Kuklia. Altogether the villages are strangely jumbled together, and must have owed their dependence to other considerations than geographical, perhaps to a classification of their products, or more probably to the fact that, after the whole island had been given away in fiefs by Guy de Lusignan, his successor Amaury only resumed a portion of these through the generosity of his vassals, and stray fiefs no doubt continuing to fall in subsequently were attached at random to various bailiwicks; had the Domain Royal been determined once for all on the first assumption of the Seignory of Cyprus by Guy, we should no doubt have had a more rational classification. The Commissioner of the district has pointed out to me that this division into bailiwicks has partly survived in the distribution of the lands of the great Tchifliks. On the fiefs see the list in Mas Latrie, L'Île de Chypre, pp. 403 foll.; and for the constituents of the bailiwicks the Italian Catalogue, printed in the same author's Hist. de Chypre, vol. iii. pp. 504 foll.

down to Old Paphos. But no one visits the villages which lie up on the hill-sides, and accordingly there is no single complete account, either archaeological or otherwise, of this fine district, known intimately by the Papho officials alone. Pococke only passed down the Ezuza valley: Engel says nothing of it, finding no data in his main authority, Von Hammer: Sakellarios seems to have travelled by Yiolou to Ktima and thence by Chrysaorgiatissa to Kykko, and to have seen nothing in the Papho villages: General di Cesnola is silent on the subject, although he marks two routes on his map of 'Travels and Explorations' which would imply that he had twice visited Chrysaorgiatissa. His foreman, Besh-besh, did a little digging in these hills, notably at Drimu, but this the General does not mention.

*Ancient copper mines.*

In the western foothills of the Forest Range more extensive evidence of ancient copper-mining may be seen than in any other part of the island: three miles to the east of Arsinoe, where the lately defunct Cyprus Copper-mining Company has been working for three years, huge mounds may be seen composed entirely of old slags, and adits have been found running for hundreds of yards into the hill-side and communicating with a labyrinth of workings now filled with water[1]. Tombs of the miners have been found near the adits themselves, and others may be seen on the hill to the west, in and about the village of Pelathousa. The vein seems to have run southwards, for great heaps of slag are to be seen again near Istingio, not far from the right bank of the Poli river: a considerable village has surrounded the workings here, the remains of which may be seen on a knoll on the left of the track to Melathia, and a number of empty rock-tombs yawn on the sides of the same knoll. A long block of stone now lying in front of the village mosque has had a piece excised from it, which the villagers declare bore an inscription: it was found in a tomb, conveyed to its present situation, and the lettered portion was cut out by a passing λόρδος. Of course my Turkish informants had no idea of the character of this lettering, but if their story is

[1] It is this vast accumulation of water which has frustrated the hopes of the modern miners, added to which expert evidence has recently declared that the percentage of copper in the ore, even if it could be ever easily worked, would not repay outlay in these times, whatever may have been its value in the days of slave-labour and greater rarity of the metal. These works are those of which Pococke heard as existing near 'Bole' (Poli). Travels, ii. p. 225.

true, we may conjecture that it was Cypriote and that perhaps Besh-besh was the abstractor, as he appears to have been in another case at Lassa on the other side of the river, and possibly both texts are among those published by General di Cesnola, and ascribed vaguely to Paphos[1]. At Melathia and Lyso are more rock-tombs, which probably belong to the same mining-population, and at the latter, which lies on the ridge midway between the two ancient mines, two stone escutcheons are built over the north and south doors of the church, and inside is a fine screen of similar (though inferior) work to that at Aschelia. The village is not mentioned by M. de la Mas Latrie as being either a fief or a part of the Domain Royal in the Lusignan period, but the presence of late rock-tombs, and early woodwork in the church point to its being a village of some antiquity. However, there is no saying from how great a distance such stones as these might not have been carried by zealous builders or restorers.

*Lyso.*

Even with the kind assistance of officials of the British Museum I have been unable to identify the coats of arms, and must leave the problem to specialists in foreign heraldry.

[1] The fact that the General has ascribed two inscriptions of Amargetti to Old Paphos (*v.* J. H. S. vol. ix. p. 262) proves that he had very little knowledge of the provenance of the antiquities collected by Besh-besh, who held a roving commission, and was the

In the other villages of this section, Myrmikoph, Steni, Peristerona, Agios Isidoros, Magounda, Kynousa, Melandra, Zakharia, Philousa, Tremithousa, Evretou and Saramá, there is nothing worthy of record: and with a passing reference to the ruined monastery of Khrysolakkona above Myrmikoph, of which nothing remains but the shell of a large church with triple apse, some traces of a cloister at its west end, and foundations of out-buildings, we may pass the Poli river and ascend the lofty ridge which divides it from the Ezuza. It is this ridge which, curving northwards, runs out at last into the Akámas, but having already described this extremity, we begin with the villages which lie just within or south of the line drawn from Cape Drepano to the mouth of the Poli river, which we have assumed to be the limit of the Akamas proper.

*Pano-Orodhes.* The first ruins that are met with lie to the east of Pano-Orodhes on the right of the path leading from thence to Yiolou; but these are mere heaps of unsquared stone, among which can be traced the foundations of a church and a circular tower, and can be of no great antiquity. A mile further east some small rock tombs are cut in the slope of a round hill, and at Miliou which lies deep down in the wooded valley of the western fork of the Poli river a few traces of ancient habitation are to be seen, to wit fragments of small columns, large squared blocks, and concrete pavement, but nothing of

real discoverer of the treasures now in New York. So much has been written and said since the publication of General di Cesnola's book as to numerous inaccuracies and misstatements contained therein, that I almost owe an apology for flogging a dead horse: but several conversations with those who had worked for him shed a (to me) new light on the subject, and showed me the genesis of much that seems mythical in the book. The truth of the matter seems to be that the General seldom directed his excavations in person, and was not present when the treasures were found; he undertook some rapid tours about the island, stopping for instance *one day only* at Old Paphos (cf. his book, p. 206, 'I superintended excavations there in 1869 for *several months*'), but his collection was amassed by the labours of his dragoman Besh-besh, both by excavation, and by purchase in the villages and in the bazaars of the towns. Thus, for example, no mention is made of Drimu in the General's book, although all the villagers aver that Besh-besh found a number of things there. The ridiculous depths to which excavations are said to have been carried, e.g. forty-one feet at Old Paphos (p. 209) in a spot at which solid rock lies only two or three feet below the surface, and forty to fifty-five feet at Amathus (p. 255) where a tomb twenty feet in depth is quite exceptional, appear to be inventions of Besh-besh's, who spent so much of his patron's money on mastica and other things unarchaeological, that he was obliged to manufacture satisfactory explanations of his large expenditure. When General di Cesnola travelled in person he knew nothing of the necessity for keeping accurate notes; in proof of this I will only call attention to his short account of the Carpass on p. 203, a most extraordinary attempt to supply the want of any certain knowledge by such vague inaccuracies as might have been picked up from merchants in the bazaar of Larnaca.

much interest. Nor has the little monastery of Agii Anargyri below the village anything to show except a hideous iconostasis painted sky-blue! I was entertained here by the *Οἰκονόμος* of the see of Papho who, after doing justice to his own cheer, proceeded to toast no less a person than Aphrodite Paphia, whose personal charms and freedom of manners he described in glowing terms. I believe that he has hopes of the episcopal throne.

*Monolith.* But on the west side of Pano-Orodhes, a mile and a half down the slope, and two miles above the Lipati site, described on page 13, is a unique specimen of the *πέτραι τρυπημέναι* or pierced monoliths, whose origin has been so much disputed. It is simply a rough mass of rock, about seven feet square, not shaped in any way by art, but pierced by the usual oblong aperture, 2 feet 10 inches in height, by 1 foot 2 inches at the lower end, which is clean-cut, and 1 foot 9 inches at the upper end which is left rough. The block has been split by natural agency, for another part lies near displaying a section of the same aperture. On the other side of a rivulet immediately opposite to this stone are remains of a small group of buildings, and a late tomb has been opened close to them; I will reserve further remarks on this variety of a large class until the description of the interior is completed, and we come to the two examples which stand upon the sea-shore below Old Paphos: but it may be said at once that this Orodhes stone seems to supply a distinct step in the evolution of the ordinary type. The ruined monastery of Agios Savas hard by has no features of interest, and I was told that a few years ago a *λόρδος* dug there and at a spot nearer to the stones, but found nothing.

*Cemeteries.* Ancient tombs have been found in various localities on this ridge; at Karydhi between Orodhes and Beyia; on the north of the village of Kathikas, and also on the west, in the latter case in considerable numbers, plain sarcophagi, cippi, local pottery, gold ornaments and glass having been unearthed by the villagers[1]. Again near Stroumbi a sarcophagus has been unearthed; an accidental landslip near Tsada revealed some poor earth graves, and the road-makers discovered others at a point north of Callepia. In none of these cases could I find any traces of a site to account for the tombs. At Polemi how-

[1] Among the glass found here was a phial in which some liquid had crystallized, leaving rings of various colours on the inner side of the glass. The peasant who found this esteemed it so great a treasure that he proposed to present it to the Queen. His loyal enthusiasm was not encouraged, and what became of the phial I never learnt, nor did I ever see it.

*To face p. 22.*

*Collotype.* *Oxford University Press.*

CELL AND CHAPEL OF THE HERMIT NEOPHYTUS.

FROM A PHOTOGRAPH BY THE AUTHOR.

ever, where two or three series of graves have been discovered from time to time in a rising ground to the south-west, faint traces remain of an ancient village on the crown of the rise: from the narrowness of the *δρόμοι* of these graves, the fragments of coarse red pottery lying near, and some jars which I saw in the houses of Polemi villagers, I had no difficulty in assigning the site to the Roman period, to which the Kathikas graves and the others above mentioned also belong: and they afford interesting evidence of the numerous population of these uplands in the days of the commercial greatness of New Paphos.

*St. Neophytus.*

In a deep valley on the western slope of this ridge lies the famous monastery of St. Neophytus, founded in the last years of the twelfth century, almost contemporaneously with the establishment of Frank rule. In sanctity it ranks in Cyprus after Kykko, Chrysaorgiatissa, and Machaeras, but in the west is the best known of all Cypriote foundations, thanks to the publication of the *Τυπικὴ Διαθήκη* of its saintly founder in 1777 at Venice, and in 1881 in the Archaeologia (vol. xlvii) from a MS. in Edinburgh. To the latter the reader is referred both for the history of the founder, and the character and circumstances of his foundation: no more instructive record exists of the original constitution of an Orthodox monastic establishment.

The present monastery buildings are situated in a little paradise of running water and deep groves of olive, pomegranate, and lemon-trees, immediately to the south of the cave in which the saint first took refuge. The latter, carved by the hands of Neophytus himself, into a dwelling room and a small chapel, is still the goal of pious pilgrimage: and except for the frescoes which have been daubed over walls and roof, remains much as its first tenant left it. In the little room, 11 ft. × 8 ft. at its largest, are his coffin-shaped bed, excavated in a recess of the rock (into which the faithful sick still climb, and turn round thrice), a little rock-cut table and seat, and over the latter a modern cupboard filled with the skulls of the hermit's earliest followers. On the seat was standing, when we visited the place, a small icon of an angel, painted on wood, certainly not in the usual Greek style, but strongly suggestive of Italian sixteenth century art; but whence it had come no monk could tell us[1].

[1] There is an Italian icon, painted on canvas, in the church of Hieroskipou, two miles east of New Paphos, and not more than four miles from this monastery. A beautiful iconostasis of Italian workmanship exists at Aschelia, two miles from

A door leads into the tiny sanctuary divided by a rock screen from the rest of the little chapel, the whole being 30 ft. long × 11 ft. broad. The roof is covered with late frescoes, the most gorgeous marking the spot where the saint upheld the falling rock with his hand. A modern porch and staircase of masonry are built on to the face of the cliff, whereby the faithful may approach this holy spot, and a second small cave has been hollowed out to the right, perhaps by one of the saint's disciples. At the foot of the cliff rises a holy spring, where tradition has it that the Virgin appeared to Neophytus.

How the monastic buildings came to be erected on the opposite bank of the rivulet, which runs down from this spring, is told us in the *Διαθήκη*, ch. xx. No church was built at first, and for some time the little rock-chapel, described above, served the purposes of the monks. The present edifice appears to be not earlier than the sixteenth century, and contains nothing whatever of interest: together with the rest of the monastery it suffered severely after the Greek rising in the early part of the present century, its books were burnt, and its frescoes defaced; but the offerings of the faithful in Greece and Russia have sufficed to restore the fabric, daub it with the usual series of frescoes, fill its screen with icons, and enrich it with silver-bound service books, and startling embroideries in gold and silver thread. The living rooms are built on opposite sides of a square, separated by a garden, and opening on to pleasant corridors which command a matchless view down the strait wooded glen to the sea nearly a thousand feet below. Blessed with a perennial spring of pure water, and with abundant shade, it is becoming a favourite summer resort of the wealthier Paphiti, and few lovelier spots could be found: but, as a monastery, it appears to be decaying fast. The Hegoumenus is non-resident, the Oeconomus is (or was) of dubious repute, the monks are very few in number, unusually rude and ignorant, and by no means observant of the rules of the Founder, especially with regard to women. (See the *Διαθήκη*, ch. xix.) Having no considerable endowment, it will fall more rapidly than Kykko, Chrysaorgiatissa, or Machaeras, into the state of desolation and desuetude which has overtaken all but half-a-dozen of the Cypriote monasteries: religious fervour is dead, and the Bishops have a direct interest in promoting the break-up of monastic

Hieroskipou, where was once a Commandery of the knights of Rhodes: and perhaps the two pictures have been abstracted therefrom.

establishments whose revenues will fall to the See; so the buildings are left to tumble into ruin, only the church and a residence for an ἐπίτροπος being kept in any repair. Nor can this fate be altogether regretted, melancholy as it is to witness the decline of ancient and once honourable foundations, and grateful as every traveller in the East must feel towards those who have so often entertained him. In a barbarous age the monasteries afforded a ready refuge to the persecuted, and sustenance to many outcasts and foundlings: in a night of ignorance and cruelty they kept alive a little flame of learning and piety: they constituted a rallying-point for the subjects of an alien power, and, inhabited for the most part by devout, if ignorant, men, maintained at least a fair name before the world. But now their day is past and the monks, knowing this, grumble at the trifling abstinence and self-denial which the rules, if properly enforced, impose upon them; their political uses are no longer beneficial, and they tend to foment intrigue: they have ceased to shine in edifying contrast among an ignorant and superstitious peasantry, for without any assistance from the monasteries the latter have in many districts progressed more than they; and, having no religious enthusiasm, the idle inhabitants of the remote cloisters give a handle to those evil reports, which weaken day by day the authority of the Orthodox Church in Cyprus.

South of this monastery the ridge begins to trend inland, and on the slopes of the bend lie a number of prosperous villages, many (e.g. Mesoyi), to judge from the rock-tombs, fragments of mouldings and so forth, to be seen in them, standing on the sites of ancient dependencies of the neighbouring New Paphos. Twenty minutes' ride above Armou lies *Armou.* what appears to be the site of an outlying villa, with some opened tombs, but chiefly remarkable for the finding of a limestone trough, shaped at one end into the semblance of a dolphin's head. The trough itself is 2 ft. 8 ins. × 1 ft. 11 ins.; but the head lengthens the whole to 4 ft. 5 ins. The basin is 1 ft. 9 ins. deep, and the whole stands 2 ft. in height. It is of very careful workmanship, the snout, ears, and crest of the dolphin being well executed, and it is probably of the Roman period. The present possessor is one Philippos of Tsada, a village on the top of the ridge three miles from Armou, and not far above the Neophytus monastery.

A mile to the south-east in a volcanic-looking valley, lies the *Marathounda.*

Christian village of Marathounda, surrounded by ruined churches. In the only perfect one—that actually in the village—is a little limestone altar, 1 ft. 3 ins. high, × 7½ ins. × 7½ ins. inscribed in half-inch letters of the later Ptolemaic period:

| 8. | ΑΠΟΛΛΩΝΙ | Ἀπόλλωνι |
|---|---|---|
| | ΜΥΡΤΑΤΗΙ | Μυρτάτῃ |
| | ΞΑΙ Ο Σ | Ξά(νθ)[ος |
| | ΥΠΕΡΟΝΑΣΑ | ὑπὲρ Ὀνασᾶ |
| | ΒΟΙΣΚΟΥ | Βοίσκου. |

The name Ὀνασᾶς occurs in a Cypriote inscription of New Paphos (Sammlung, No. 30) and elsewhere (cp. Pape s. v.), and Βόισκος twice on pedestals found by us at Old Paphos (J. H. S. vol. ix. 57, 99). This designation of Apollo is new, and recalls in form the best known Cyprian epithet of the god, ὑλάτης. A third epithet—Melanthius—was found at Amargetti, about five miles distant from this point, and I conjectured in the Journal of Hellenic Studies (ix. pp. 171 foll.) that it embodied a village name. I should prefer however to revoke that conjecture now, and place the two epithets Melanthius and Myrtates on the same basis without giving them any local signification.

It will be noticed that all these three epithets of Apollo suggest a reference to the vegetable kingdom. Apollo ὑλάτης is Apollo 'of the grove'; Apollo μυρτάτης may be he of the myrtle; and Apollo μελάνθιος recalls the medicinal attributes of the herb μελάνθιον, a species of poppy, known to botanists as *nigella sativa.* The close connection of trees and plants with the Greek divinities is well known, and several were often associated with a single god, for example the ivy and vine with Dionysus, and the myrtle, apple, poppy and rose with Aphrodite: and in a few cases they have supplied distinctive appellations for their patrons;—the tamarisk gave Apollo the epithet μυρικαῖος in Lesbos and the Thessalian Corope, and the myrtle itself that of μυρτῷος in Cyrene[1]. A very curious example occurs in Cyprus itself, tending to prove that the custom of so naming obtained in the island, to wit the Aphrodite μυκηρόδις 'of the almond tree,' commemorated in an inscription of Melusha published by General di Cesnola (p. 423, no. 23).

The *healing* powers ascribed to Apollo would account for the

[1] The authorities for these epithets are quoted in Ritter and Preller, Griech. Mythologie, p. 292, 4th ed.

bestowal of such epithets as μελάνθιος and μυρτάτης, if they are really derived from the melanthium and myrtle. The virtues of the former and of its oil are set forth by Dioscorides (iii. 92; I. 46); it appears to have been accounted potent against an amazing variety of disorders, such as headache, toothache, the itch, eye complaints, tumours, worms, bites of spiders, difficulty of breathing and affections of the urinary organs. The properties of the myrtle are described by the same author (i. 133) in almost identical terms, eye complaints, headache (after wine), spider bites and urinary affections all appearing once more; and it is worthy of remark in connection with the last class of disorders that many of the objects found at the seat of Apollo μελάνθιος (Amargetti) displayed conspicuous phalli, either on statuettes or cones. In one case we found a bronze representation of the complete organs. But yet these were not so much ithyphallic or exaggerated as faithful attempts to reproduce the membra; and I am inclined to believe that they were ex voto offerings dedicated, after cure by the virtues of the μελάνθιον, in a shrine of Apollo the Healer[1]. It is quite to the point to compare[2] with the epithet the names Μέλας and Μελανεύς, given to a son of Apollo, king of the Dryopians, by Pherecydes (Schol. Soph. Trach. 354) and Pausanias (iv. 2. 2) respectively; but these names must be themselves explained before they can be used to elucidate the meaning of μελάνθιον, and they may very well be due to the medicinal virtues of some *black* berry, similar to that of the Cyprian herb. But at any rate they tend further to show that μελάνθιος is not a local epithet, but is the outcome of a connection of Apollo with black colour.

It seems probable then that the Cyprian Apollo was essentially the physician. His cult in the island was not very important; beside these two villages of Amargetti and Marathounda, we hear of it in ancient times at Tembrus, Erystheia, and Amamassus[3], obscure townships probably in the neighbourhood of Curium, and of course at Curium[4] itself the fountain-head of the worship. Here it was located at a spot known as Hyle, a town according to Stephen of Byzantium, but probably only a sacred grove, where arose a temple, iden-

[1] Compare with this the cult of Apollo Lermenus on the Upper Maeander (J. H. S. viii. pp. 376 foll.) where the god is the healer after he has taken vengeance on impurity.

[2] As Dr. Deecke kindly suggested to me.

[3] Steph. Byz. s. vv., Nonnus Dionys. xiii. 445.

[4] Strabo, 683 c.

tified by General di Cesnola with a spot now called 'Apellon' some hundreds of yards inland from Curium itself. Julian[1] alludes vaguely to Cyprian altars dedicated to Helios and Zeus, but seems to distinguish the former from Apollo. On coins the god appears at Curium, Paphos (Nicocles II), Salamis (Nicocreon) and Soli[2], but except in the first case (?) not before the fourth century. As for inscriptions, a cave now known as *ἀλώνια τοῦ ἐπισκόπου* is dedicated to Apollo Hylates near New Paphos, and two dedications have been found to the same god at Drimu. General di Cesnola found several dedications in Cypriote to him at Athieno[3]; a sanctuary of Apollo was revealed near Voni in the district of Kythrea, five years ago[4], and a fragment of a bowl was found near Tamassus in 1887 bearing portions of the words *ἀνέθηκε Ἀπόλλωνι* on the lip. An interesting variety occurs in a Cypriote inscription of Pyla[5]—Apollo *μαγίριος*.

It is noteworthy that in none of these localities is there any sure evidence of a very *early* cult: the coins and inscriptions referring to Apollo are not earlier than the fifth century, and many, e.g. the New Paphos dedications, are of the fourth: and this accords with the inference to be drawn from the long exclusion of the Greek alphabet from Cyprus, to wit, that western influence was hardly felt in the island at all until the fifth century. Western settlements there were, such as Marium, and perhaps Salamis, but they affected the general condition of the island as little as did the Phoenicians of Citium and Idalium. As research has tended more and more to minimise the part played by the latter in Cyprian economy, and to reject their claim to be the importers even of the great goddess of the island, or the founders of her temples[6], so western influence must be relegated to the days of Evagoras. Not until the end of the fourth century do we find the *first* Cyprian inscription in Ionian letters.

[1] Or. iv. p. 135, Spanh., quoted by Engel, p. 664.

[2] Head, Hist. Num. pp. 622 foll.

[3] Sammlung, Nos. 72, 75, 77, 78.

[4] M. O. Richter in Mitth. des deutsch. arch. Inst. ix.

[5] Sammlung, No. 120, and also Moriz Schmidt Die Inschr. von Idalion, p. 98.

[6] It will be remembered that we found *no* Phoenician relics at Old Paphos at all; nor have any been found at Amathus, Salamis, Lapethus, or indeed (except isolated instances) anywhere but at Citium and Idalium. Has the Phoenician question been revised since the days of Engel, when the Cypriote script was supposed to be Phoenician? If the latter people did so much in Cyprus how came its script to survive? and why should not the goddess have come originally from the same source as the script?

Of the character of the cult we are only told that all who touched the altar near Curium were hurled from the cliffs; but certain other facts should be noticed as throwing a side-light:—Apollo μυρτάτης, if he be 'of the myrtle,' encroaches on the domain of Aphrodite, to whom that tree was especially sacred. Among the objects found at the seat of Apollo at Amargetti were a great number of doves or of statuettes holding doves, the bird of the Paphian queen; and it certainly appears that Apollo chose for his chief abodes in Cyprus the preserves of the latter, the Western or Paphian district, and the neighbourhood of Golgoi (Athieno?) the predecessor of Paphos according to Pausanias. Was he then partly confused after his introduction into Cyprus with that type of masculine beauty which accompanies the Asiatic Goddess in all her wanderings, either as son, lover, or slave, under the names of Adonis, Linus, Tammuz[1], Cinyras, Attis, and so forth? Indeed it would have been very difficult to keep the two types of beautiful form apart in a semi-oriental island. If this were so it would reasonably explain two perplexing points about the Amargetti antiquities: firstly, the mixed character of the emblems unearthed—doves, phalli, cones, bunches of grapes or berries; and secondly, the strange dedication ὀπάονι μελανθίῳ found in twelve out of fifteen inscriptions from the site; for this might well be Apollo in the part of *servant* or inseparable attendant on the Paphian queen whose shrine is only twelve miles away. He would thus combine the Greek attribute of healing, to which perhaps the phalli belong, with those of fertility (the cones on the one hand, and the grapes on the other), and procreation (the doves?) belonging more peculiarly to the Asiatic Goddess[2].

I venture therefore to put forward the view that Apollo, μυρτάτης and μελάνθιος, is the Healer by the virtues of herbs, rather than the vague shepherds' god which I proposed in explanation of the Amargetti problem. It precludes also the necessity of inscribing on the map of ancient Cyprus two villages, *Myrte* and *Melanthus*, for which no other authority whatsoever exists. If ancient names must be found from Engel's

[1] Note the occurrence of his name at *Tamassus*, perhaps the city of Tammuz. That Apollo and Tammuz were identified in Cyprus is, I believe, the view of Herr M. O. Richter.

[2] If Engel's conjecture (ii. p. 668) that it was the Argive Apollo ἐρίθιος, who was introduced into Curium, and that he is identical with the Rhodian ἐριθύβιος, 'the averter of blight,' be ever substantiated, it will fit in with this Amargetti cult of the Healing-fertilizer very well.

list, perhaps *Μυρικαί*, a *χωρίον ἱερόν* according to Hesychius, and recalling the Lesbian Apollo *μυρικαῖος*, and *Πάνακρον* (Nonnus xiii. 446 "*τέμενος βαθύδενδρον ὀρεσσαύλοιο Πανάκρου*": and Steph. Byz. s. v.) suit two seats of Apollo better than any others not yet attached, but which should be given to which, I will not pretend to conjecture.

*Episcopi.* A winding track, descending for two miles among the eastern spurs of the ridge, leads to Episcopi[1], a village on the Ezuza itself. Late Roman remains are all that are to be seen here: on the summit of a cliff which overhangs the village are the foundations of a group of buildings, proved by the presence of oil-receptacles and a mill-stone of black basalt[2] to be those of a farm. South of the church of Agios Archangelos in the village itself two plain marble columns of 1 ft. 2 in. diameter project five feet from the ground, but are evidently not in situ: and in Ktima I was shown by M. Cleoboulos a bronze figurine from this village, similar to those found by us at Amargetti. As no ancient remains are visible at Marathounda, it is possible that the Apollo Myrtates altar, described above, has come from Episcopi.

We have now fairly rounded the elbow, and can follow the ridge inland up the right bank of the Ezuza. Once more ascending the long slope to a point near Tsada, and passing the disestablished monastery of Stavros Mythas (where MM. Beaudouin and Pottier appear to have found a Cypriote text, published in the Bulletin de Corresp. Hellénique, vol. iii. p. 350, but which I failed to see), we come to the pretty village of *Callepia.* Callepia, half hidden among groves of pomegranate, acacia, olive, and arbutus. The church has both the reputation and the appearance of great age, and was formerly dependent on a monastery whose ruins are to be seen north-east of the village: the massive walls and narrow deep-set windows speak of a different period to that of most Cypriote churches, and I searched among the piles of mouldy service books rotting in the corners, with some hope of lighting upon MSS., but could

[1] Distinguished in Lusignan times as Episcopi Cordechu (or Cordudu) from the larger village nine miles west of Limassol (Mas Latrie, Hist. de Chypre, iii. p. 507). It was part of the Domain Royal, and pertained to the bailiwick of Aschelia.

[2] Precisely similar to that figured by M. Rénan, Mission en Phénicie, Pl. V, No. 1. Another specimen lies between Amargetti and Limona; and a receptacle in which such stones worked may be seen at Limnia, near Salamis. There is no reason to suppose that any of these or M. Rénan's example are of an early period, or purely Phoenician, but the coincidence on the two coasts is interesting.

only find a few tattered leaves of a fifteenth century *Μηναῖα*. However, seated upon the top of the apse outside is a much older relic, a headless limestone statue, unearthed somewhere and brought here, no one could tell me when. The statue, in its sitting posture and without the head, is two feet high, draped and apparently female, though so much weathered as to show very little indication of sex: the right arm from the elbow rests on the right thigh, the hand lying palm downwards on the knee while the left hand rests between the breasts. This latter feature recalls the well-known attitude of the Asiatic goddess clasping her breasts with both hands, and it is possible that the Callepia figure is that of the Paphian Aphrodite in her oriental character of a goddess of fertility:—but the style and drapery are not of an early period.

The village lying next in order up the valley, Letymbou, is famous in all the country side for its churches; three only, those of Sts. Kyriakos, Theodoros, and the Panagia Photolampousa, are in a state of repair, but the crumbling remains and sites of no less than seven others, four dedicated to the favourite Cypriote saint, St. George, and one each to St. Marina, St. Epiphania, and to the Holy Ghost, may be found among the sixty or seventy houses of the village. The most interesting is that of St. Kyriakos, whose frescoes are of truly remarkable beauty in such a land of daubs as Cyprus: those on the transept-roof represent scenes from the life of our Lord, those on the roof of the nave and choir a legend, probably of St. Kyriakos; and in all there is a freedom of attitude, beauty of expression, and richness of colouring which I have seen nowhere else in Cyprus. I could only regret that there was not with me someone with greater knowledge of fresco painting, who might have said with authority that which I suspected, namely that this church has been decorated by Italian artists, and was a Latin edifice. The villagers have repaired the fabric, but the frescoes are fast falling to pieces, and something ought to be done towards their better preservation. In the Lusignan period Letymbou was a *cazal* of the bailiwick of Emba[1]; and a document published by M. de la Mas Latrie (iii. p. 235) shows that it was a centre of local government; for certain 'jurés' seem to have existed here, one, Vasili, paying 100 besants on appointment. These were assessors of the local court of the bailli and,

*Letymbou.*

[1] Mas Latrie, Hist. de Chypre, vol. iii. 507.

corresponded, according to M. de la Mas Latrie (iii. p. 813), to the bourgeois of the Viscount's Court; they are also known at Alona near Morphou, and their presence seems to argue a position of importance for Letymbou in the Frank period, of which its crumbling churches are a survival.

*Dhrys Stavrolivanou.* Between this and Polemi is the largest tree in Cyprus, a great holm-oak, known as the *Δρῦς Σταυρολιβάνου*, standing alone in the middle of a little plain. I put the tape round it five feet above the base and found it to measure 23 ft. 6 in. in girth, while the span of the branches was 118 feet. Among the great claws which it throws out on every side nestle the ruins of a tiny church, still enclosing a *προσκυνῆσις* or rude altar [1].

*Drimu.* Among the many villages which dot the eastern end of the ridge only Drimu has any reputation as an ancient site. Four Cypriote texts are ascribed to it in Collitz' Sammlung, Nos. 26–29, which prove that it boasted a worship of Apollo Hylates; these texts are said to have been unearthed by a shepherd in a locality nearly a mile to the north of the village and not far from the ruined church of Agios Minás, where also Besh-besh dug and found, according to native testimony, many terra cottas, statuettes, etc. I picked up a few fragments of such, but concluded from the nearness of the bed-rock that the place was not worth further excavation. Near the ruined church are three large blocks of limestone, with singular perforations: the largest is four feet high, rudely shaped into an almost conical form and has two holes near the apex; another is also rudely conical and has one perforation, similar to those in the great Kuklia blocks, and apparently bored to facilitate traction from the quarry. Being found also in Gozo and on other Phoenician sites, their presence may be taken as proof of the work of the latter people, and in this case as confirming the evidence of the Cypriote texts as to ancient settlement here [2].

[1] These rude piles of stones are built up and still venerated on the sites of hundreds of churches which have long ago fallen into ruins, and the Cypriote is never at a loss to ascribe the holy spot to a particular saint. On the patron's festival a little incense is still burnt there, and the ashes placed on the altar in a potsherd. When no stone of the walls remains upon another, loose stones are collected and piled up rudely in the outline of a church.

[2] There seems no reason to doubt the genuineness of these Drimu texts in spite of the suspicious circumstances connected with certain others, said to have been found here afterwards, and (probably) identical with those published by MM. Beaudouin and Pottier (Bulletin de Corresp. Hell. 1879, p. 347). M. Aristides Michaelides informed me that the shepherd, whose sheep had accidentally scratched out the first, saw that there was money in such discoveries, and forged others, selling them, as I understood, to Aristides himself, who presumably showed transcripts of them to the

Perhaps they are the remains of a *τέμενος* of Apollo Hylates on the present site of the church. A white marble basin, now used as an oil-receptacle at Dhrynia, a mile and a half distant from Drimu on the other side, may also have come from here: it is 2 ft. 9 in. in diameter and quite plain except for three string mouldings running round the top, and being of foreign material can hardly be modern. *Dhrynia.*

Nothing else in this section is worth mention from an archaeological point of view except a cippus built into the church fence at Melia near Dhrynia, and inscribed with the single word *Melia.*

9. ΕΥΧΗΝ *εὐχήν.*

In every other village on this ridge I halted at one time or another but found no antiquities: in Anadhyou, I heard the usual story of a written stone carried off ten years ago by a *λόρδος*, who, if he be not fictitious, was probably Besh-besh; and in a field near Kritou Marottou, one Ioannides Parthenius, a monk of Chrysaorgiatissa resident in the village, declared that strange things had once been found: but I knew too much of this gentleman's inventive powers to place much credit in a statement which was designed to attract the Excavation Fund to Kritou.

Descending from Kritou Marottou to Kannaviou we pass the river not far below the point at which it debouches from the Forest, and climb the tremendous slope of the Panagia mountain, the culminating point of all the Papho ranges. It is sanctified at this day by the presence of Chrysaorgiatissa, the second monastery in Cyprus, on its northern slopes a few hundred feet only below the *ἀετοκρημνός*, as its flat cliff-girt summit is called. It must have been sanctified in former days by the Temple of Hera which appears to have existed a mile to the west of the monastery on a site now covered by the church and quadrangle of Agia Moni, a beautiful little *μετοχή* of the greater foundation of Kykko[1].

Two inscriptions in the Cypriote character were found among the foundations of the church when it was in process of restoration in 1885, and, with a third in ordinary Greek, were built into the west wall on either hand of the doorway. The Cypriote *Temple of Hera.*

French students; why he did not show the stones themselves, may well be asked. In any case two facts seem to stand out: first, that the Bulletin inscriptions are probably not genuine: secondly, that M. Aristides Michaelides knows more about them than anyone else.

[1] On the Ordnance Survey map it is mis-called 'Chrysiaorgiatissa Mon.' as though it were a *μετοχή* of the neighbouring foundation.

ones were copied by M. Vondiziano of Limassol and entrusted to Dr. Deecke for publication, and they appeared in the Beiträge z. Kunde d. indg. sprachen, xi[1]; but owing to the imperfect copies from which Dr. Deecke had to work, he could not be certain of the last two lines of the longest of the two texts, and rejected the name *Ἥραι* as not suitable to the spacing or probable in itself. However, I was more successful than M. Vondiziano in getting good impressions of the stone, and both in squeeze, photograph, and copy *Ἥραι* is beyond doubt. As further there is an entirely new form in line 4, and my copy supplies several other missing characters, it is perhaps well to re-publish the inscription in facsimile. It is the most accurately and elegantly cut Cypriote inscription with which I am acquainted: the characters are 1½ inches in height, exactly proportioned and spaced, and remarkable for a slight broadening at the extremities, a fashion designed (like the addition of apices) to give a finished appearance. We might therefore conclude at once that this inscription, like the similar one at *Ἁλώνια τοῦ ἐπισκόπου* near New Paphos, is of quite the latest period, viz. the end of the fourth century B.C. The material is fine limestone, the surface being accurately dressed; water has trickled down the centre and worn the face, but with two exceptions the characters can all be read. In one end of the block is a semicircular excision.

10.

O · pa · po · pa · si · le · u · se · ni · ko · ke · le · ve · se ·
o · i · e · re · u · se · ta · se · va · na · sa · se ·
o · pa · si · le · (vo) · se · ti · ma · ra · ko · i · ni · se ·
ta · se · ki · (?) · na · u · (?) · ne · a · se ·
ka · te · se · ta · se · ta · i · te · o · i · ta · e · ra · i ·

[1] I was not aware of this when I visited Agia Moni, and imagined that I had found something entirely new; nor did I learn my mistake until Dr. Deecke himself, to whom I had sent a squeeze, pointed it out to me.

'Ο Πάφω βασιλεὺς ΝικοκλέϜης
ὁ ἱερεὺς τᾶς Ϝανάσσας
ὁ βασιλέϜος Τιμάρχω ἶνις
τας . . . . . . . . . . . .
κατέστασε τᾷ θεῷ τᾷ "Ηρᾳ.

The value of the fourth symbol of line 4 I cannot determine, nor can anyone to whom I have submitted it; it is perfectly clear on the stone and my photograph and squeeze: the latter I sent to Dr. Deecke, and he replies: 'Der Abklatsch ist durchweg sehr deutlich. In z. 4 ist Ȳ = Ki; ⧖ vermag ich nicht zu deuten: es scheinen mir dann zu folgen die Reste von na · u · ? · ne · a · se · Das ne · ist ıϟı. Wie aber das Ki · ? · na · u · ? · ne · a · se zu deuten ist weiss ich nicht.' Prof. W. M. Ramsay suggested to me that τάς is followed by some long feminine compound of κίων: if so, ⧖ might represent *jo*, for which no symbol is yet known.

The other inscription is cut in a much inferior style, the characters being 2½ inches in length, narrow, deeply and coarsely incised. The face of the stone has been plastered in modern times. Its wording is identical with the former up to the word τας, at which point the stone has been sawn across. I have no doubt also that the text, published in the Sammlung (No. 40) and vaguely ascribed to 'Paphos,' was impounded by the Turks from this site[1]; and the τᾶι θεῶι mentioned in it will be accordingly not Aphrodite but Hera.

Dr. Deecke conjectured that this King Nicocles is identical with the one dethroned by Ptolemy Lagus in 310 B.C., and this accords with the late appearance of the lettering of the first inscription. It should be noticed, however, that the only *certain* inscription referring to him (J. H. S. vol. ix. p. 239) is in ordinary Greek character.

11. The third inscription is in the Greek character, but so much worn as to be quite hopeless. It is built into the wall low down on the left of the door. The lettering is coarse and of the fourth century B.C.; I give as much as I was able to decipher in repeated attempts on the stone and squeeze.

[1] The ἐπίτροπος and several peasants told me tales of previous finds on this spot.

ⱵΥΟΙ /·///·/// Σ //· ΤΙ /·//·//·//· Ο ΙΙΙ Λ Α /·//·//·/·
Ν Ν Ν ///////////////////////////////////
//·// Γ //////////////////////////////////
// \ Δ F Λ Ο /////////////////////////////
////////// Ο Η Τ Ω Μ · ////////////////////
/// Ͱ Ο Τ Ω Ν Κ Α ' /////////·//////// Ο ///
///·// Ρ Γ Υ Ρ Ι Ο Ν Π Ι . .  // Τ ///·/ Ε Ι Σ/·////·//·/
//·/ Α Υ Τ Ω Σ Δ Ε Λ Ͱ Ν /////////////////

Except some part of (ἀ)δελ(φ)ός in line 4; a participle, e.g. (ἐστρατηγη)κότων καὶ, in line 6; (ἀ)ργύριον in line 7; and (ὡσ)αυτῶς δ' Ἕλεν(ος)? (cf. Inscr. of Paphian Temple, Nos. 11, 20, 109),—nothing else is worth conjecturing.

In the neighbourhood I found other traces of the temple, whose ruins probably lie buried beneath the monastery buildings. Built into a fence on the north of the church are four plain limestone drums, 2 ft. 2 in. in diameter, and the same in height; and it should be noted that these are nearly as large as the drums in the southern stoa of the temple at Old Paphos. A drum of 1 ft. 9 in. diameter lies near them, showing that two orders of columns existed. In the apse of the church itself, and in a confining wall to the south of it are many large blocks, conspicuous among the small rubble of which the rest of the church and the buildings near are constructed; the church itself has the reputation of being one of the oldest foundations in Cyprus, and the apse is probably part of the original structure.

Without excavation no more can be known about this temple of Hera, and from the circumstances of the site a thorough exploration can hardly be made. Terms might however be arranged with Kykko with a view to making a few borings in the open spaces on all sides of the church, which probably stands on the temple itself.

The importance of this shrine may be inferred from the royal dedications, and the size of the columns. It was situated in one of the most favoured spots in Cyprus: the cliffs of the ἀετοκρημνός close round it in a half moon, averting every wind but the west, and from their foot gushes a perennial spring, famous throughout the district for its purity; as it flows down the slope its course is marked by orchards and olive-groves, and the flowering shrubs gave forth a scent almost overpoweringly sweet on the June evening on which I first rode into this happy valley. Lying nearly 3000 feet above the sea it enjoys cool airs in the hottest summer, and the view over the Papho ridges to the Bay of Poli and the Akamas, and up the Ezuza valley to the shaggy heights of the Forest, is of singular beauty. Claudian might have seen such a spot, and made of it his 'Venusberg[1].'

The ascription to Hera is of great interest in a part of the island devoted to Aphrodite. So essentially Hellenic a goddess must have come late to Cyprus, and perhaps this temple was only erected in the fourth century B. C. by this King Nicocles whose name appears in all its inscriptions; even Apollo ought to be her senior in the island, for the settlement of Curium gives a definite period and reason for his introduction, and, as I have conjectured, his easy assimilation with Asiatic divinities would tend to spread his cult. But Hera had no such sponsors, and probably was not known in Cyprus until the Hellenising period which followed the introduction of Athenian influences in the middle of the fifth century, and culminated under the rule of Evagoras at Salamis in the early part of the fourth. Her individual cult was never popular; indeed we have further evidence of it only at Old Paphos and Amathus: in a fragmentary inscription built into the church of the Panagia Chrysopolitissa at the former her name appears after *Ζεὺς Πολιεύς* and Aphrodite[2], and at the latter another inscription (C. I. G. 2643) makes mention of a Heraeum.

Of the great monastery of Chrysaorgiatissa this is not the place to speak at length, although no very adequate description exists[3]. Unfortunately there is no compilation treating of it like the Patriarch Ephraim's history of Kykko, or the Ritual Ordinances of Nilus of Machaeras, or St. Neophytus, but I was fortunate enough to procure from the monks an engraving, made for the Monastery in 1801 by one Cornaro, a *Chrysaorgiatissa Monastery.*

[1] Epithal. Honor. et Mar. 49 ff.

[2] This inscription, very imperfectly read by Engel's authorities and by Cesnola, is published more correctly by M. Waddington (Lebas and W., No. 2795). It runs according to our reading :—

. . . . . . . . . . . .

*Αἴ[γ]υ[πτ]ο[ν] τὸν μαντιάρχην καὶ τὸν ἀδελ[φὸν τὸν δεῖνα ἱερέα Ἀφροδίτης καὶ Διὸς Πολιέος καὶ Ἥρας φιλαγαθία[ς ἕνεκεν τῆς εἰς ἑαυτούς.*

[3] Sakellarios (vol. i. p. 111) says so little about it, that one wonders if he was ever really at the place. Pococke missed it, lying the night at Agia Moni. Miss Agnes Smith (Mrs. S. S. Lewis) stayed there in 1879 ('Through Cyprus,' pp. 170 foll.).

Cretan artist, and detailing in a series of tableaux and legends the *ἱερὸς λόγος* of the holy picture to which the sanctuary owes its origin and present fame,—but from what authorities this was compiled I know not. According to this account the picture was painted by St. Luke and found its way to Isauria; on the breaking out of the *εἰκονομαχία* it was thrown into the sea by a woman and wafted across the strait to Cyprus. As it lay on the beach a monk, Ignatius, was directed to it by a vision, and bore it into the mountain of *Roia* (presumably the Panagia hill, or a general name for the Forest Range), where his comrades received it, and built for it a shrine, the germ of the present monastery of Chrysaorgiatissa. This occupies four tableaux, the remaining six being devoted to miracles wrought subsequently by the picture, or generally by the Virgin on behalf of Cypriotes, none being of any interest.

It follows that the authorities (if any) on which this is based placed the foundation of Chrysaorgiatissa in the middle of the eighth century, for the mention of the *εἰκονομαχία* and Isauria probably contains a reference to Leo the Iconoclast (717–741). If this be true (and there seems to be no reason why it should not be so) Chrysaorgiatissa is by far the oldest of the great monasteries of Cyprus, the foundation of Kykko falling in 1092, that of Neophytus at the very end of the twelfth century, and that of Machaeras in 1200. The sanctity of its picture was somewhat dimmed by the importation of the great Eleousa of Kykko, but has always been very great, and still attracts numerous pilgrims; indeed it is popularly supposed that he who for seven years in succession has visited both Kykko and Chrysaorgiatissa on September the 8th, the day of the great common *πανήγυρις*, has performed the equivalent of a journey to Jerusalem; for between the two shrines lies a six hours' journey through the Forest. Chrysaorgiatissa has also a smaller *πανήγυρις* on August 15th.

After the occupation of Cyprus by the Turks, the monastery suffered severely through the appropriation of its lands by those of the conquerors who hastened to settle on the pleasant Panagia hill; at this day there is not a single purely Christian village in its neighbourhood except Statos, whereas Lapithiou and Kannaviou are wholly Moslem, and Pano Panagia very nearly so. In recent years its finances have been mismanaged, and the remnants of its real estate have been sold or heavily mortgaged, so that at present, with the possible exception of Trooditissa, it is the poorest of the greater monasteries of

Cyprus; however under its new Hegoumenos, one of the most energetic and capable ecclesiastics in the island, it should recover its prosperity. It has about a dozen monks all told, of whom only four were in residence during my stay; but the number of *δοῦλοι* seemed considerable.

Architecturally the buildings present no points of interest; much damage was done to them some sixty years ago after the Greek rising, and they have been since restored. They are grouped irregularly about the church and have evidently grown by accretion. The church has the usual gilt iconostasis, and beautiful silver hanging lamps and censers; in the gallery at the west end is kept a library, which I searched thoroughly without finding anything better than an illuminated vellum MS. of the Gospels, looking not earlier than the fourteenth century; but the monks showed no desire to part with this, and it was not worth haggling over. The other MSS., about seven in number, were either *Μηναῖα* or books of music. Of the holy picture I was only permitted to see a square inch. On the whole Chrysaorgiatissa lacks interest: it has less of the dignity of an ancient foundation than Kykko, and less life than Machaeras; though it excels both in the natural advantages of climate, water, and scenery. Years of depression, and the want of rational occupation such as is provided by the management of large estates, have produced a slipshod untidiness in the monks and the buildings: but under vigorous administration the monastery will doubtless resume its proper place among the great sanctuaries of the Orthodox Church.

The remaining objects of archaeological interest to be found in the villages of this section demand only a brief enumeration.

*Lapithiou.* A small late site, marked by squared stones, two plain shafts and an uninscribed cippus, lies near the ruined church of Agia Paraskeve, half-a-mile below Lapithiou: it can have been no more than a large farm, but an ingenious Turk, with an evident eye to future profit, declared that the village hodja knew of a spot, where might be found a subterranean church whose floor was of silver and its roof of gold! Surely we would come and dig there next year? At Agia Varvara above the same village are two deeply buried monoliths, which, if excavated, would probably prove to be the usual *πέτραι τρυπημέναι*: near them lies a large 'oil-stone[1].'

[1] As for convenience I must use this term frequently without explanation, it may be well to state at once that it means the class of large circular stones, often seen on

*Agios Photios.* Descending the western slopes of the hill, and passing Statos, the village of Agios Photios is reached, and in the cornfields below are two similar monoliths, called by the villagers Ἁγίαι πέτραι: the one is embedded up to its perforation, but still stands 6½ feet above the ground: the other remotely resembles the Orodhes examples in being hardly shaped at all—a mere block of natural rock through which a slit has been driven; it only stands 4 feet high and is not more than six inches thick. Near it are traces of poor foundations, and two plain shafts of small diameter. A stone basin, evidently an oil-receptacle, was found near it and now lies in the village, and some poor graves have been opened in the slope immediately above. Coarse red potsherds lie about in profusion. In a vineyard on the ridge above the village terra cottas are said to have been found, but the ancient site seems to have lain immediately to the east of the present Agios Photios and about the ruined church of Agios Prodromos: here are many traces of buildings, plain shafts, and two more monoliths, the one very small and nearly wholly embedded, the other not pierced quite through, as is the case also with an example in the Kostithes valley (*v. infra*, p. 48).

*Phallia.* On a spur of the mountain below Agios Photios lies Phallia, whose inhabitants are of gipsy origin, unless my judgment is much at fault. No other village in Cyprus shows the same peculiar type, particularly noticeable in the women, who appear, though Moslems, not only to dispense with veils, but to accost and talk openly to a stranger in the company of the men. I have noticed an equal pitch of freedom only in the remote Moslem villages of the Carpass, whose inhabitants are certainly not of Turkish origin. These Phallia ladies wear also a profusion of gold ornaments, unique in Cyprus. The faces of both men and women are of extreme swarthiness, the hair is raven-black, the noses and lips fine, the eyes very brilliant, and the ears small. There is a slight resemblance to the Marathasiotes, who are believed by the Cypriotes to be descendants of Phoenician settlers, but on the whole the likeness is rather to the gipsy type with which we are familiar in the west. A few poor graves are said to have been opened here, but nothing worth recording was found; and the same is true of Choulou, *Choulou.*

sites in Cyprus, whose grooved surfaces show that a mill-stone has worked upon them to crush olive-berries. They are larger than those now in use, and belong to days of greater wealth.

a large and rascally village at the foot of the mountain, where I bought two jars of Roman period and a terra-cotta mask.

Pentalia, on the slope overlooking the Xero, can show poly- *Pentalia.* chromatic local pottery of a slightly better order, obtained recently from tombs in the chalky cliff overhanging the village: and on a knoll, a few minutes' ride below, are remains of a village-site, several small drums of 1 ft. 5 in. diameter, oil-stones, and foundations covering the hill-side. Remains of a precisely similar character exist also a mile to the south, not far from the Adhia tchiflik; and passing these the traveller reaches Agia Marina, whose church boasts a carved iconostasis *Agia Marina.* vastly superior to the conventional Cypriote type, but so far inferior to the Aschelia work that one hesitates to call it a Latin remnant; the same qualification applies to an elaborately-carved picture-frame in the church of Natan, in the Xero valley some *Natan.* four miles south of Agia Marina: in both the design is a simple floral one, but the relief is high and executed with a care foreign to native art. No record exists of either village in the Lusignan period. Tombs have been found at the latter. In the hills above lies Amargetti, already sufficiently described in the J. H. S. vol. ix. pp. 171 foll.

Facing about we ascend the course of the Xero, past the Sinti monastery with its large empty church, and under the eastern flanks of the Panagia hill, to the little hamlet of Vretsa, not yet acknowledged as a 'village': thence a path leads up the narrow gorge of the river into the Forest itself, and the last outpost of civilisation is a little mill, known as Roudhia, the *Roudhia mill.* property of the Kykko monastery. Into the front of this has been built a sculptured stele, where found and by whom brought hither I could not learn: it represents two female and a male figure draped, rather more than half-length, and two feet in height. Those on the right and left grasp the hands of the central figure, that of a young girl, in the conventional manner of leave-taking, and the monument was probably raised to a daughter by her father and mother. The clumsy lines of the drapery recall the statuettes found in profusion at Amargetti, and the relief is undoubtedly of a late period. The material is native limestone. Any interest that this stele possesses arises from the remoteness of its present situation: no ancient site exists nearer than Agia Moni, but it is hardly credible that this heavy stone (2 ft. 10 in. × 3 ft.) should have been conveyed eight miles, and down two thousand feet to be built into a mill! I questioned the monks at Kykko as to its history but in vain.

The mill stands on the left bank of the Xero, at the foot of the narrow ridge which intervenes between this stream and the Dhiarrizos. In the villages of this fourth section I found no antiquities whatever worthy of record: a Cypriote inscrip-

*Salamiu.* tion is published in the Sammlung, No. 41, as from Salamiu, a village high up on the ridge, some thirteen miles inland as the crow flies, but I visited the place twice, without seeing or hearing of any remnants of the temple of Horus mentioned in the inscription, or of any other relic of antiquity; and perhaps the provenance of the inscription is wrong. The neighbourhood is chiefly remarkable for magnificent olive-trees of great age—in themselves a proof of ancient settlement.

*Nikoklia.* Nikoklia, which appears to preserve the name *Νικοκλῆς*, common in the Cinyrad dynasty of Old Paphos, only a mile away[1], encouraged hopes, but yielded nothing.

*Praetori.* The fifth and last section, which contains Old Paphos itself, is almost equally barren. Praetori, far up towards the Forest, can show some empty Roman tombs at a spot called *Ἕλληνες*, midway between itself and Yerovasa, and on the path to Kedhares. A jar of common local ware, and a figurine from a vase, were sold to me in the village, and probably came from these tombs. In a field half a mile below Praetori lies a rough column, similar to the Paramali stone inscribed in honour of Jovian, but on this there is no lettering, and it was perhaps a boundary mark.

*Arsos.* On the top of the ridge and on the eastern slopes towards the Kostithes lie the great wine-villages of Arsos, Vasa, and Omodhos, the richest of their class in Cyprus. The first-named was, as Arsinoe, the residence of the exiled Orthodox Bishop of Paphos in the thirteenth and fourteenth centuries, but has nothing to show for it but the fine church of St. Philip.

*Vasa.* Vasa was a fief of the great house of Ibelin, Counts of Jaffa, and perhaps owes its present wealth and prosperity in the first

*Omodhos.* instance to the premier barons of Cyprus. Omodhos boasts a

[1] It is very possible that the name *Kuklia*, whose derivation has been much disputed, is merely a corruption of this, the original, form. Other derivations, less satisfactory, have been suggested (see J. H. S. vol. ix. p. 191). We must suppose that Νικόκλια retained its name from very early times, and that, when the modern village grew about the ruins of Old Paphos, desolated by the exodus under Justinian II and by the fleets of Haroun al Raschid, it took its title in a corrupted form from the nearest existing village. The plural form τὰ Κούκλια τῆς Πάφου tells, however, against this suggestion.

fine but desolate monastery, enclosing a famous church, the *Σταυρὸς 'Ομόδου*: the guest-chamber is a pretty room adorned with good native carving of modern date, and in the church are preserved certain fragments of cord, said to be the remnants of those which bound our Saviour, and to have been presented by the Empress Helena.

*Yerovasa.* Only Yerovasa has anything of greater antiquity to show, and even this amounts to no more than a group of *πέτραι τρυπημέναι.* Above the village near the path to Arsos are three, two fallen and one upright, and all of great size: but half a mile to the west, on the edge of the Dhiarrizos valley is a more interesting specimen, canonized as Agia Trypiméne; near it stands on edge a manifest 'oil-stone,' and a small stump of wood stands opposite the perforation on one side, and is now covered with rags, the repositories of fevers. Of the many monoliths about Dhora and further down the Kostithes valley Dr. Guillemard has treated in the Athenaeum of April 14, 1888.

There remains then to be described only the strip of flat coast-land which intervenes between the earlier and later capitals, and included two towns known to Strabo, *'Ιεροκηπία* and *'Αρσινόη*, and one important mediaeval village, Aschelia.

*Hieroskipou.* The first-named, as is well known, is the present Hieroskipou, a village two miles east of Ktima, which boasts some indifferent gardens in a little valley leading from the spring, but nothing of that singular beauty which impressed General di Cesnola twenty years ago. No traces of ancient buildings are visible in the neighbourhood, but some florid Corinthian caps of greyish marble in the precinct of the church, the hind-quarters of a marble horse in the village-spring, and many Graeco-Roman gems found in the fields near, bear witness to Strabo's accuracy.

*Arsinoe.* Arsinoe is more difficult to identify: Aschelia on the left bank of the Ezuza suggests itself as the mediaeval representative of an ancient town, but, although there are many relics of the Knights of Rhodes in the two churches, the aqueduct, and the foundations of the château at that village, there is absolutely nothing classical, and furthermore it stands fully a mile and a half from the sea, whereas Arsinoe seems from Strabo's expression to have been situated on the shore itself. The ancient geographer places it west of the promontory of Zephyria, which is itself west of Old Paphos; now this headland is unquestionably the modern *Ζέφυρος*, the rocky point which runs out immediately to the west of the mouth of the Xero, and east of a little bay, the only one before New Paphos is reached, and still a favourite anchorage for caiques. In the hollow of the bay, near the solitary church of Agia Evrésis (or Agia Ircóna ?), are faint traces of an ancient site: remains of walls cover the sides of the knoll on which the church stands, and the latter itself seems to be built on older foundations and of old material, fragments of white marble being embedded in its walls. Inside is a very fine 'oil-stone' of coarse pinkish marble, now serving the purposes of an altar. Between the church and the sea is a well, once plastered, and hard by large squared blocks. To the west is an ancient quarry of considerable extent, and to the east a tumulus, and a curious mass of rock pierced in all directions by tunnels, roughly hewn and vaulted. One such tunnel is as much as 150 feet in length, and all are now used to stable flocks at night; and I can only suggest that in former days they served the purposes of warehouses or of a covered bazaar, and had been excavated to this end: in any case they are not natural and are clear proof of ancient settlement at this point.

This is all that exists above ground, but enough in my opinion to fix the site of the '*ἄλλη Ἀρσινόη*' of Strabo, mentioned by him only[1], and probably of little importance. Of its *ἄλσος* no tree remains.

*Aschelia.* The mediaeval settlement of Aschelia[2] has been alluded to already; as the centre of the great sugar-growing plain of Cyprus, it was constituted the head of a bailiwick of the Domain Royal, and on the capture of Acre the Hospitallers received lands in its neighbourhood, and established there a Commandery. It is now a miserable hamlet, of not more than half-a-dozen families, but its two churches preserve relics of former

[1] Arsinoe seems to have been a singularly common city-name in Cyprus, for there were at different times no less than four:—(1) The best known of the name, the city on the gulf of Poli, whose site is now covered by Poli-tis-Chrysochou; the city existed previously to the period at which it was called Arsinoe, but under what name is uncertain (see *infra*, p. 105, for the theory that it was formerly called Marium). (2) On the east coast, south of Famagusta (Strabo 682. 3). This is generally accepted as the see of the Greek bishops of 'Arsinoe' (Gams' Series Episc. eccl. Cath. pp. 438, 439), and not Poli-tis-Chrysochou, nor Arsos, as M. de la Mas Latrie thinks (Hist. i. p. 80). (3) The one mentioned in the text. (4) The present Arsos, in the south-east corner of the old kingdom of Paphos, to which the Greek bishop was banished in 1222 (*v. supr.* p. 4). This was probably a Byzantine foundation.

[2] Chielie in a Latin declaration of James the Bastard (Mas Latrie, iii. p. 176), and l'Eschelle in French (ibid. iii. p. 219), the latter being the equivalent of La Scala or 'the Port.'

*To face p. 43.*

*Collotype.* *Oxford University Press.*

PULPIT AT ASCHELIA.

FROM A PHOTOGRAPH BY R. ELSEY SMITH.

prosperity: the smaller lies a quarter of a mile to the south of the present road, and is a small Byzantine edifice, completely ruined; it contains however a fine cap of white marble, elaborately moulded, and a tombstone also of white marble, in the centre of which appears a lion passant with an indistinguishable object at its head, the bearing of some Hospitaller. The larger lies close to the road itself and contains the finest carved woodwork in Cyprus. The following account of the church and its contents has been communicated to me by Mr. R. Elsey Smith, with whom and Mr. M. R. James I visited it on more than one occasion.

'The church inside, not including the apse, measures about 62 feet by 19 feet; it is covered by a continuous pointed stone vault, divided into four bays, rather than supported, by three transverse moulded ribs springing from moulded corbels at a height 10·90 feet only from the floor. The side walls are 3·80 feet thick, and opposite the ribs external buttresses 3·70 feet wide and projecting 1·60 feet, give additional strength, and the roof shows no signs of failure.

In the first bay from the west end, an exceedingly light arch has been thrown across to assist in carrying a gallery which has a separate door in the south side. The springing of this arch is 6·95 feet from the floor, and the rise is only 1·75 feet, while the voussoirs of which it is composed are but 1·00 foot deep; it is a dangerously light bit of construction, and has failed slightly in the centre though it still stands apparently secure, but the gallery above has been removed. In the second bay the side doors occur, and in the thickness of the south wall a narrow flight of steps leads up through the jamb of the door to the pulpit which is placed exactly in the centre of the south wall. This is a remarkable specimen of wood-carving, but appears to have been constructed out of an older carved frieze. It projects from the side of the wall, and is formed by five sides of a regular octagon three of which are most elaborately and finely carved. The centre (the left-hand side in the photograph) it will be observed is in two pieces, which are placed in their right position, while the panels on either side, only one of which is seen, are each in a single piece though badly split, and have been placed vertically instead of in the horizontal position for which they were designed. The subject of the frieze consists of birds and animals and a magnificent running scroll of the most richly carved foliage. The design is very vigorous, the execution in high relief, but carved with the utmost delicacy and attention to detail without however any loss of breadth. When fitted up as a pulpit two additional plain sides were added, and a moulded cap and moulded and carved base, while the soffite was inlaid with wood in geometrical lines. The wood is of a dark rich colour, and appeared to me to be chestnut. It is a fortunate circumstance, now that it is in Greek hands, that, owing probably to the poverty of the district, this and the other carving in the church have never been painted. In some of the Nicosia churches, where carved work of somewhat similar character exists, its appearance has been almost ruined by successive coats of paint, and especially by the red, blue, green and gold of the last coat.

The Rood screen stretches right across the church just east of the third vaulting rib, that is to say in the fourth bay. The height exclusive of the cross, but including the two steps on which it stands, is about 15·00; it is divided into three unequal stages. The lowest is 7·20 feet high to the bottom of the first horizontal carved frieze, and is divided vertically into seven bays, of which the central is the widest. These are separated by elaborately carved pilasters, with caps having somewhat of a Corinthian character, and have semicircular heads supported on small carved brackets, which in the centre bay are formed by birds with spread wings devouring bunches of grapes; the heads are moulded and fringed with delicate interlacing cusps, and the spandrils filled in with carved scroll work. Above this is a frieze 1·00 foot deep and tilted forward, of carved scroll work divided into three parts by two carved tablets placed immediately over the two central pilasters, and the whole is surmounted with a moulding. The central opening has two richly carved doors treated with arches and gables, having a more strongly marked Gothic feeling than the rest of the screen. They give access to the sanctuary and altar, the other openings had merely a cross rail 0·30 feet deep at a height of 3·45 feet from the floor which is richly carved; the part below this rail is now filled in with plain vertical boarding, the upper part with Greek paintings of saints.

The stage immediately above the frieze is divided into fifteen compartments by pilasters whose height including cap and base is 1·65 feet. Above the pilasters are a series of semicircular heads with the interlacing cusps, and surmounted by rather flat gables, the whole elaborately carved on a rail 0·90

To face p. 45.

Collotype. Oxford University Press.

BALDACHINO AT ASCHELIA.

FROM A PHOTOGRAPH BY R. ELSEY SMITH.

feet deep, very considerably tilted forward, and forming another strong horizontal line. The openings in this stage are all filled in with boarding.

The top stage is somewhat similarly treated, but is divided into thirteen bays only, and is somewhat higher, measuring with the topmost cornice or frieze about 3·20 feet, though the exact dimension could not be ascertained; this also was filled in with boarding, and from the top of the cornice over the centre of each panel there is a long projecting bar, fantastically carved, apparently in imitation of a Gothic gargoyle.

The whole is surmounted by a cross reaching to within a few inches of the crown of the vault, and with ropes of flowers and foliage carved in wood on either side. Though an excessively rich piece of work, this appears a trifle over-elaborated, and somewhat large for its position and the size of the screen and church; whereas in the screen itself, although the carving is most elaborate, it is not in very high relief, and is contrasted with large masses of plain woodwork, and produces a very handsome, but not overladen, effect. The whole of the work is strongly framed together, the framing appearing at the back, but being partially hidden in front by the carved friezes, canopies, &c.

Lastly we have the Baldachino, another elaborate and exquisite specimen of woodwork. Owing to the want of space it was impossible to photograph the whole of it, and the fragment, which shows about half the east side, was only obtained by holding the camera outside the small window in the apse.

The lower part is rectangular and plain with square angle posts, and measures 3·60 feet in height to the top of the altar slab under which a cupboard is formed; above this point the posts are carved; at a height of 1·50 feet above the slab there is a moulded and carved horizontal band; up to this level the posts remain roughly square, but above it they become circular and are treated with large spiral coils, between which delicate sprays occur with branching leaves and flowers, and every here and there a bird with carefully executed plumage; the height to the top of the cap from the altar slab is 4·75 feet, and to the top of the moulded cornice 5·10 feet, while the cap is 0·70 feet high. Between the columns on the long sides there occur very flat cusped arches moulded and carved, and with a delicate carved edging, the spandrils being filled in with pierced and carved work consisting of flowers and foliage. In each spandril is the representation of a bird with wings spread, and wearing a crown or crest; birds also are found at the centre of the arches.

The cornice is surmounted with flattish carved pediments of which a mere fragment is seen.

The preservation of the whole of this carving is very remarkable; with the exception of the splitting of the panels in the pulpit and the loss of a few portions from the screen, it seems to have suffered no damage whatever, and to be as sharp and perfect as when first erected in the church.

It seems possible to fix the date of its execution within somewhat narrow limits; it is clearly Renaissance in character, and can therefore be little, if at all, earlier than the commencement of the sixteenth century, while in the middle of that century the last of the Hospitallers, by whom the church was probably erected at a not much earlier date and adorned with this exquisite work, were expelled by the Ottoman invaders. It appears, therefore, to belong to the early years of the sixteenth century, and this well accords with the character of the work, for we find marked signs that Gothic influence had not been entirely shaken off. This is observable especially in the folding doors of the central opening of the Rood screen and the curious gargoyle-like projections higher up, and in the treatment of the flat cusped arches of the Baldachino [1].'

*Monoliths.* Lastly, following the coast line eastward towards Old Paphos we halt before the two great monoliths, standing between the mouths of the Xero and Dhiarrizos, which Von Hammer (Topogr. Ansichten, p. 144 sqq.) believed to be the relics of a harbour (which never existed), while General di Cesnola's luxuriant imagination reconstructed from them a Temple of Aphrodite Anadyomene (Cyprus, pp. 213 foll.), at which the pilgrims from New Paphos halted before ascending to the greater shrine of Aphrodite Paphia. To his measurements the reader is referred, but not to his picture, for the latter is somewhat imaginative, the stones really standing over 200 yards from the beach, and the background of serrated peaks dropping to a commonplace ridge not a thousand feet high. In their present condition the stones are about eleven feet in height, three feet broad at the top and five feet where they disappear into the

[1] Since this account was written I learned that the whole of the carvings had been purchased by an English resident in the island, Mr. J. W. Williamson, who has now brought them to this country: at the present moment their ultimate destination is uncertain.

*To face p. 46.*

*Collotype.* *Oxford University Press.*

MONOLITHS NEAR KUKLIA (PAPHOS), LOOKING SOUTH-WEST.

FROM A PHOTOGRAPH BY R. ELSEY SMITH.

soil, and two feet thick. The eastern one of the two is perhaps older—at any rate far more weathered—than the other, which has modern foot-holes cut in one edge, whereby women may climb upon it for the cure of barrenness. Each has a slit driven right through the stone, three feet in length by one foot three inches broad, and they stand side by side (the slits not facing) six feet apart. Near them are lying a cippus and many squared blocks and drums of small plain columns of late date.

General di Cesnola is not the only traveller who has sought a religious explanation for these monoliths; they have been constantly regarded as menhirs, emblems of fertility, whose conical shape and apertures were designed to combine the organs of the sexes, counterparts of Jachin and Boaz in Solomon's Temple. Lately Dr. F. H. H. Guillemard, in the Athenaeum of April 14th, 1888, has propounded a far more prosaic theory, that they are the remains of ancient presses, whose use the modern Cypriote has forgotten: with this I concurred in a postscript to his letter, and now, on a still wider experience of similar stones, see no reason to change my view.

The religious theory depended very largely for attractiveness on the supposed singularity of these Paphos monoliths, and their existence only near the Temple where Aphrodite's emblem was undoubtedly a conical stone. But Dr. Guillemard and myself have found over forty similar stones in all parts of Cyprus, a list of which I append:—

5 on the plateau near the village of Anoyira (*v.* Athenaeum article).
6 in the Kostithes valley, near Anoyira, three on each side of the river (*v.* Athenaeum article).
4 on the village site, known as Agios Stefanos, near Pakhna (*v.* Athenaeum article).
1 on the site known as Despoticos, near Pakhna (*v.* Athenaeum article).
1 between Pakhna and Agia Evresis (*v.* Athenaeum article).
1 in the Kostithes valley, near Dhorá (*v.* Athenaeum article).
1 on the hill behind Pissouri.
4 near Agios Photios, on the Panagia hill (*v. supra*, p. 38).
2 (?) near Lapithiou, on the Panagia hill (*v. supra*, p. 37).
4 near Yerovasa (*v. supra*, p. 41).
? 1 near Giaz—seen by Dr. Guillemard later.
1 in a field a mile and a half east of the large Paphos monoliths.

1 near Orodhes (*v. supra*, p. 20).
1 near Kolossin.
4 on the site known as Pergamon, near Akanthou (*v. infra*, p. 97).
6 on that of Macaria (*v. infra*, p. 103).
1 between Agia Grosh and Agios Epiktetos, Kyrenia.
4 recorded by General di Cesnola in the Carpass and at Cape Greco.

These, with the two Paphos stones, make up a total of fifty.

Dr. Guillemard has stated the characteristics of this class of monoliths and their surroundings most clearly and concisely, and I need do no more than record the most significant, in the main drawing on his account, and supplementing it here and there in the case of such stones as he did not see.

The monoliths are of all sizes, from the great Paphos examples down to the one at Agios Photios only 4 feet high, and they face impartially all points of the compass: with one exception, that at Pissouri made of conglomerate, they are cut from the ordinary limestone of the island. The dimensions vary indefinitely and show no significant coincidences. They are found generally singly, sometimes in groups of two or more, but in only *two* cases, Paphos and Pergamon, do two stand in close proximity, and in the latter only do they *face* each other, i. e. with the slits opposed. This slit is in almost every case driven horizontally through the stone, carefully finished, from 2 to 4 ft. long by 9 in. to 1 ft. 6 in. broad, and either rounded or square at the top: in a very few instances its lower end slopes, as if for convenience of tilting something passed through; and three stones are not completely perforated, two being near Anoyira and one near Agios Photios: to this significant fact I will recur presently. All the monoliths are shaped more or less exactly, tapering in some cases slightly to the top, which is either rounded or square,—with the exception of the examples, mentioned on pages 20 and 38, at Orodhes and Agios Photios, which are mere masses of untrimmed native rock, and are possibly the oldest specimens existing.

There is thus every kind of minute variety and very little indication of character in the monoliths themselves: but their surroundings and 'properties,' as Dr. Guillemard has shown, are more instructive. They stand in many cases at the corner of a platform of masonry or rubble, apparently intended to resist weight or pressure, and near them are often foundations of small many-chambered buildings, like those of a farm. Near the platform cisterns often occur, lined with cement, or cut in the solid rock, and small gutters lead into them: this is especially noticeable near the Pissouri, Pergamon, and Agios Stefanos stones. Dr. Guillemard also found fragments of stone vessels about 10 in. deep, and of large terracotta jars, as much as 3 ft. 4 in. in diameter at the mouth, similar to those used for storing wine and oil at this day. These were in all cases of coarse unglazed red ware which might have been of any date. Dr. Guillemard also noticed certain cut stones near a few of the monoliths which he likens to the uprights of a modern oil-press, but I did not see the instances in question, and must refer the reader to his article.

But the most significant adjuncts of many of the monoliths are two varieties of mill-stones, the one circular, hollowed out to a depth of 5 or 6 inches, and manifestly worn by a roller circulating from a peg in the centre (such a roller of peg-top shape was actually found in some cases); the other, not hollowed, but seamed with channels diverging from a flat boss in the centre to a runlet round the rim, which finds outlet at a spout. On such a stone at the present date olives are pressed, after being crushed on the first mill-stone by the circular roller: and there can be no manner of question that, in calling both these kinds of mill-stone ἐλαόμυλοι, the peasants are perfectly correct [1].

All the surroundings, therefore, of the monoliths point to their being connected with olive culture; but it is not easy to determine the part played by the upright pierced stone itself in the operations of crushing or pressing. As Dr. Guillemard has shown, the crushing is done by means of a beam with the roller attached, made to revolve from a peg in the centre of the circular stone; and in this operation the monolith could not be needed. It must be connected, accordingly, with the *pressing*, and be a relic of days before the modern *screw* was invented, and the operation had to be effected by simple impact of weight or of a lever. This would amply account for the modern Cypriote's ignorance of the character of the monoliths. Unfortunately no parallels exist in any of the countries of the Levant: the many varieties of ancient press seen by M. Rénan in Syria (Mission

[1] One or other, or both, of these mill-stones accompany nineteen out of the fifty monoliths that we have seen, and many others may exist unperceived among the dense scrub which often surrounds the sites.

en Phénicie, passim) were rock-cut indeed, but presented no other points of resemblance: and only the occurrence of remains of wine-presses and circular stones near certain of the so-called 'menhirs' of Moab (Conder, Heth and Moab, pp. 253, 254) makes one suspect that some of these mysterious stones are not unconnected with the press. It is at least curious that the Hajr-el-Mansûb, near which lies 'a large wine-press,' should have a mysterious groove 6 in. wide and 1½ in. deep cut across its face; and that the Arabs should give to a large group of 'menhirs' and 'dolmens,' three quarters of a mile away, the name 'mother of little olive trees,' and declare that it was once an oil manufactory.

The function of the monolith I conceive to have been something like the following: through the perforation was passed a massive baulk of timber, to one end of which was suspended a ponderous upper mill-stone: to the other end, projecting beyond the monolith, would be attached ropes, whereby that end might be pulled down, and thus the mill-stone at the other end *up*: the latter could then be lowered at will 'with a run' on to the olive berries lying on the nether stone[1]. To resist the strain of alternately raising and lowering such a beam with such a weight at the end, a very massive fulcrum would be required, and this was supplied by the monolith, whose long slit allowed for a good deal of 'play.' The latter was at first made horizontal, but later the slope was introduced for convenience of tilting the beam: in these cases the press would be on the side towards which the slope falls. The three imperforate stones present a difficulty; and I can only suggest that, if they are not (as is likely enough) simply unfinished specimens, they represent feeble first attempts before even the advantage of using the stone as a fulcrum was recognised: the beam was simply rested in the 'step' afforded by the imperfect perforation, and the stone at its extremity was lifted and dropped by men working under the beam. At the best, however, it was a clumsy contrivance enough, and must have been at once abandoned and soon forgotten on the introduction of the screw-press: but this was probably not until Byzantine times, to judge from the pottery and other remains which lie near so many of the monoliths. It is however possible that the new process would continue to be employed on the same sites as the old

[1] Compare the principle on which the shadouf bucket was raised and lowered in ancient times, and is still in Egypt and Asia Minor.

beside the now meaningless monolith, until the exodus under Justinian II., 688 A.D., robbed the island of half its inhabitants, and left so many villages and farmsteads to fall to ruins in a deserted land.

The modern Cypriotes have utilised a few of the mill-stones, but the majority are much larger than those in use nowadays, and thus have remained in situ: the uses to which the monoliths were once put they have absolutely forgotten (as they have forgotten other obsolete things much more recent, e.g. the cultivation of the sugar-cane on the Paphos plain), and their ignorance has invested these solitary relics of a past age with properties attractive, but misleading, to the student of folk-lore.

I have already mentioned the Agia Trypiméne near Yerovasa, round which bushes and stumps bear countless rags, whereto countless fevers and agues have been consigned; and the perforation of one of the Agios Stefanos stones was full of vicarious pebbles, while the apex of another was similarly loaded. This custom is, no doubt, at least as old as the Mosaic scapegoat, but is of so universal acceptance in the East (nor altogether unknown in the West) that a special origin need hardly be inferred for it in particular instances. I have observed rags tied to trees and shrubs, not only near this monolith, and the dolmen, known as Phaneroméne, near Larnaca, but to many other trees and bushes near nothing in particular, both in Cyprus and Asia Minor. In two cases only could I hear of a habit of crawling through the aperture for the cure of sickness: ailing children are said to be passed through the Paphos stones, and barren women through one of those near Anoyira: and on the top of one of the former women sit, as on the holy stone at the Trooditissa monastery, and on many stones in Egypt and elsewhere. Troth is also said to be plighted by clasping hands through the slit at Paphos, as in the Woden stone in Orkney. The natives of Agios Photios call their monoliths vaguely ἁγίαι πέτραι, but I could elicit no trace of any belief in their possessing medicinal or other virtues; and a similar result attended my constant and persistent enquiries as to all the remaining examples in Cyprus—that is to say, that to not one fourth part of the whole number of instances does any popular superstition attach. For example, the villagers of Kalorgá smiled at the suggestion that there was any virtue in the six monoliths of Macaria, and to one only out of twelve near Anoyira was any sanctity attributed. Several stand near churches, as at Anoyira, Kolossin, and Pergamon, but it is just as probable that the village press was erected, as the oil and wine presses are invariably at this day, near the church (because in its vicinity lay always a piece of undisputed common land), as that the church rose beside an old monument of phallic worship. In short, the belief in the mysterious virtues of these monoliths exists in so few cases, and is so weak even in those few, that it may fairly be argued that it is only of modern origin and has not had time even yet to develope into a universal tenet.

## CHAPTER II.

### THE CARPASS.

*Scenery and people.*

THE name 'Carpass' has been used in ancient and modern times to denote the long peninsula, which, projecting towards the mouth of the Orontes, forms a vast breakwater to the Bay of Salamis and Famagusta. From its base at Trikomo, it runs out for over forty miles without exceeding eight miles in breadth, while in two places it is contracted to less than two and a half: and to this singular position between two neighbouring seas, whose airs temper the summer heat, to its superb scenery, and its simple, thrifty peasantry it owes the peculiar charm which all travellers appreciate who, like myself, have just left the torrid Mesaoréa.

So dense a forest as that which clothes the Vallia and the regions east of Rizo-Karpaso is seen nowhere else in Cyprus: dwarfed, indeed, by the lightness of the soil and want of rain, the shrubs and firs composing it cannot compare tree by tree with the pines of the western mountain ranges; but the undergrowth of the Carpass is denser, and better able to survive the heat of July and August.

The grandest scenery is to be found at the root of the peninsula, where the last peaks of the Northern Range, densely wooded and riven into wild forms by the torrents, terminate at Yioudhi in the sea itself. Thenceforward a lower mountain system runs up the promontory, abrupt and deeply scarred on the northern side, but leaving flat forest tracts along the southern shore, or opening out a series of fertile valleys and plains such as those of Agios Theodoros, Gastria, or Sykadhes, east of Galinóporni. No other part of the island is so extraordinarily varied, albeit everything is on a small scale; little plains green with cotton-fields and melon-gardens, hemmed in by sheer crags; flat-topped ridges, stony, and thick set with forest; peaked hills, bare from foot to top; then other smiling plains, and so on. Everywhere from the central ridge the Karamanian Taurus, from Tarsous to Annamur, lies full in view, and from the eastern hills the peaks of Casius may always be seen; while looking back over Cyprus the eye wanders round the great bay of Salamis to a horizon bounded by Mt. Sta. Croce and the peak of Machaeras, seventy miles away.

The coastline is bolder and more broken than elsewhere in the island, and, added to the wildness of the forest tracts behind, gives a singular beauty to the scenery. On both sides of the promontory rocky bays and islets succeed one another, very different to the even sweep of the southern coasts: no one of these bays could be made of service for modern shipping, but in the days of vessels of small size and draught, the harbours of Aphendrika (Urania), Agios Philonos (Carpasia), Exarchos, Makhaeriona, Gialousa, and many more on the north coast, must have been much frequented by the traders of Asia Minor. Indeed the chain of Byzantine and mediaeval remains noticed by M. de la Mas Latrie[1], as existing on the Karamanian shore, and used by him as evidence of a great mediaeval commerce between the two coasts, finds its exact counterpart in the series of stone-strewn sites, occurring at every few miles from Moulos (Macaria) to Cape St. Andréas.

Probably this facility of communication with the outer world, coupled with comparative isolation from the rest of Cyprus, has imparted to the peasantry of the Carpass their peculiarly un-Cypriote look: the white skins and frequent fair hair, the beauty of the women[2], and the use of foreign words such as '*τρέ*' for *τρεῖς*, *ῥιδάλλα* (rix-dollar?) for a coin, suggest that Western influence is here especially present[3]. The Mussulmans who inhabit the central villages of Agios Andronikos, Elisis, Korovia, and Galinoporni present few of the ordinary characteristics of the Turk: they speak Greek and are almost ignorant of Turkish; the women rarely veil themselves, but, on the contrary, stare at and speak to the western stranger in the presence of the men; while the latter show little of the reticence and reserve which mark the Moslem elsewhere. The industrious habits of both Turk and Greek, their assiduous tillage of the soil, and careful husbanding of what small portion of water the sun allows to them in July, the good construction of their houses, and the comparative cleanliness of their habits, may be

[1] L'Île de Chypre, Souvenirs Historiques, p. 230.

[2] Cf. Mrs. Scott-Stevenson's remarks, 'Our Home in Cyprus,' p. 294; and for an opposite view, Sir S. Baker, 'Cyprus as I saw it in 1879,' p. 139.

[3] Can these Carpasiotes be the descendants of the 'Veneziani bianchi,' who sprang from the soldiers of Vital Michaele, settled in Cyprus after the first Crusade, and were still a distinct race in the thirteenth century? (Stubbs, Lectures in Mediaeval Hist. viii. p. 189.)

ascribed as much to these causes, as to favourable climatic conditions, and to the undoubted fact that, owing to its inaccessible position, the Carpass was allowed to retain under the Turks some of that prosperity which had been the common lot of the whole island under the Frank rulers [1]. At least it is certain that no district so much impresses the traveller with its good government, order, and essentially native civilisation as this remote peninsula.

The name by which it is still known is of great antiquity; for the foundation of *Carpasia* is lost in the obscurity of heroic times, and its inhabitants have always been called *Καρπασεῖς* or *Καρπασεῶται*. Demetrius of Salamis who writes *Καρβασία*, derives it from the wind *Κάρβας* [2], known also at Cyrene, but as to whether this was a name for the east or the north-east wind, authorities differ. *History.*

A short notice in Strabo[3] furnishes the only description of the Carpass which any author of antiquity has left to us; but, the geographer besides enumerating the towns of Aphrodisium, *Ἀχαιῶν ἀκτή*, and Carpasia with its harbour, tells us no more than that the transit from the last named to the Carpasian isles was only 30 stadia (not far wrong); that the eastern end was mountainous; and that on its extreme point stood the temple of Aphrodite Acraea, '*ἄδυτον γυναιξὶ καὶ ἀόρατον*.'

Could the earliest history of the peninsula be recovered, it might prove of great interest; for it is most probable that this end of Cyprus was the first to receive that immigration from Cilicia which has left so strong an impress on the whole island. Indeed the legend that Teucer, the immigrant from Asia Minor, landed in the Carpass may represent this tradition.

As soon, however, as we are on firm ground, the Carpass has lost its individuality in the larger aggregate of the Kingdom of Salamis, of which it must have formed about one third part. Scant authority exists whereby to determine the boundaries of the Cyprian Kingdoms, either early or late, but the Carpass, and the whole eastern portion of the Mesaoréa, including the district of Cape Greco, must always have appertained to that of Salamis, which, according to M. Six[4], included at one time or another Chytri (Kythrea), Ledra (Nicosia), and even Tamassus itself, at the foot of the western mountains. It is improbable however that it passed the Northern Range, as does the

[1] See Mas Latrie, Hist. de l'Île de Chypre, ch. iv. p. 98.

[2] See note in Engel, vol. i. p. 84. Demetrius is quoted by Steph Byz. s. v. Καρπασία

[3] xiv. 682.

[4] Revue Numismatique for 1883, p. 254.

modern administrative district of Famagusta, for the natural boundary is too well defined; and therefore I have assigned in my map the eastern end of the northern strip of plain to the Kingdom of Kerynia, whose territory must have lain almost wholly to the east of itself, since Lapethus, ten miles to the west, was also a royal city[1]. That Aphrodisium ever had an independent king, or was a royal city in any sense, is proved neither by numismatic nor any other kind of evidence that I can discover[2].

The large towns of Carpasia and Urania probably existed from early times as the principal ports of the district, receiving much commerce from the Asian coasts, and acting as outlets for Salaminian trade, if the timid mariner feared to double the cape of Dinaretum. To judge from the ruins at the apex of the Vallia, an important town must have guarded the northern limit of the Salaminian Bay; and somewhere on the northern coast between Aphrodisium and Carpasia stood Teucer's landing-place Ἀχαιῶν ἀκτή. The extreme point of the long promontory has been rendered famous by the mysterious temple of Aphrodite Acraea. Lying actually within sight of the Syrian coast, the Carpass must have been harried by many a Phoenician fleet during the next century and a half, while the kings of Salamis alternately maintained and lost their independence, and probably it suffered severely during the ten years that Evagoras was shut up in his capital. After the kingdom of his successors had been subjected to the Egyptian Empire, we hear definitely of an invader landing in the peninsula,—no other than Demetrius Poliorcetes, who crossed from Cilicia, drew up his fleet at Carpasia, and, having harried the country, took by assault both that city and Urania, before marching to commence the siege of Salamis, and fight the greatest naval battle of antiquity[3].

Thenceforward until Christian times we hear nothing of the Carpass, as distinct from Salamis: we may infer that the Jews, who destroyed the latter, and devastated its territory in the reign of Trajan, did not spare these fertile coasts; but we have no certain knowledge of any event previous to the foundation of a bishopric at Carpasia, still situated probably on the sea-shore, and not yet forced by piratical and Arab incursions to remove to the central ridge, and become the modern Rizo-Karpaso; indeed, the ancient church, whose ruins overlook

[1] See Diod. xix. 79.

[2] The conjecture that it is the Upri' whose king paid tribute to Assyria has not met with acceptance.

[3] Diod. xx. 47.

the old harbour, is dedicated to the sainted founder of the see, St. Philo. His life and therefore the foundation of the bishopric falls in the latter half of the fourth century A. D.; during the absence of St. Epiphanios in Rome in 382 A.D., he was left to administer the metropolis of Constantia with power to ordain[1], and he became known to fame as the author of a commentary on the Song of Songs. Thenceforward, the name of the see appears regularly in Hierocles and the Notitiae, and Constantine Porphyrogenneta ranks 'Carpasus' among the thirteen chief towns of the island.

At some period of Byzantine rule, perhaps after the recovery of the island from the Arabs by Nicephorus (964 A.D.), the castle of Kantara or the Hundred Rooms (ἑκατὸν σπίτια) was built on the last lofty peak of the Northern Range[2] to keep watch and ward against the corsairs who infested the strait of Kerynia; to their attacks the long Carpass was especially vulnerable, and Pococke tells us that even in his day it was sorely harried by the Maltese[3]. In the fourteenth century the Carpass was a fief of the family of La Roche, but for how long a time previously it had been in their possession we have no evidence,—possibly since the partition of the island by Guy de Lusignan himself in 1192. In any case a certain Gauvain de la Roche, son of the Seigneur of the Carpass, was among the adherents of Henry II in 1307[4], and in 1364 the wife of Afre (?) de la Roche was almost captured by the Saracens, who made a raid on the peninsula during the absence of King Peter I in Europe, and of his fleet at Adalia: but the vigorous measures taken by the prince of Antioch precluded a renewal of the disaster. If a tombstone found by M. de la Mas Latrie in the mosque of Emerghié in Nicosia, and recording the death of Marie Antiaume, wife of 'Sire Rovo de Carpass,' in 1388, be correctly read, it would seem that the La Roches had ceased to rule at Rizo-Karpaso at the end of the century, but the French savant confesses to

[1] Dict. Christ. Biog. s.v. and the Preface to his Cant. Cantic. in Galland, Bibl. Vet. Patr. ix.

[2] M. de la Mas Latrie by a strange and rare slip ascribes its construction to the Lusignans (Les Comtes du Carpas, Bibl. de l'École des Chartes, vol. xli. p. 375), although in his History (vol. i. p. 12) he has rightly stated that, like St. Hilarion and Buffavento, it was in existence when Richard of England landed, and, according to Roger de Hoveden (Rolls Ser. iii. p. 111), opened its gates without resistance. If Roger de Hoveden means to imply that Richard received Isaac Comnenus' surrender *in person* at Cape St. Andréas, he probably visited Cantara also in person *en route*.

[3] Travels, vol. ii. p. 218.

[4] On the whole Frank régime in the Carpass, see M. de la Mas Latrie's admirable article in the Bibliothèque de l'École des Chartes, quoted above. My facts are all derived from him.

doubts as to the word 'Rovo,' and suggests La Roche. In any case by 1467 the seigneury had passed to the De Vernys, (who had perhaps held the neighbouring fief of Agridia near Aphendrika since the thirteenth century), for it was from a certain Louis de Verny that James the Bastard received it in that year, either in virtue of an exchange, or by confiscation; but on the death of Louis in 1468, his son Aguet received it again at a rental of 1000 byzants, and the king presently added to it the transport animals and oxen of the cazal[1].

Thus far it had been merely a seigneury, but in 1472 Aguet de Verny was apparently deprived, and Jean Perez de Fabrice, an Arragonian, already high in favour with King James, Admiral of Cyprus, and Count of Jaffa, was further created Count of the Carpass, and premier baron of the island: the latter title he appears to have held in virtue of his titular fief of Jaffa, but it pleased his successors, the Giustiniani of Venice, who had lost the latter, to assert that, contrary to all ancient usage, the premiership depended on the comté of the Carpass, and not on that of Jaffa, of old held by the great house of Ibelin, and now by the Venetian Contarini, who had received it at the hands of King James' widow, Catherine Cornaro, with the sanction of the Republic of Venice. For the details of this squabble which gave employment to two families and the Council of Ten as late as 1568 (only three years before the fall of Famagusta), I must refer the reader to M. de la Mas Latrie's article, only stating that the advantage was always on the side of the Counts of Jaffa, and that they at last gained a decisive verdict; only in 1538 and 1539 did Angelo Giustiniani succeed in procuring illegal enrolment at the head of the Cypriote barons.

The fief had passed to the Venetian family on the death of Jean Perez's unmarried son in 1510, through the marriage of his sister Charlotte to Nicolas Giustiniani. The comté of Jaffa had already been taken away in 1474, and was never again claimed with any insistance by the Giustiniani, of whom four in succession were Counts of the Carpass. Their history, so far as known, is a mere record of squabbles with the Contarini: their revenues are stated in an Italian inventory printed by M. de la Mas Latrie (Hist. vol. iii. p. 490) to have amounted to 2500 ducats per annum, inferior to those of the Cornari and Contarini; and their authority extended especially over Rizo-Karpaso and Agios Andronikos, and generally over the whole

[1] These documents are printed in Mas Latrie's Hist. de Chypre, iii. pp. 245, 260.

peninsula, while attached to the fief was also a knot of villages in the Kythrea district of the Mesaoréa, of which Knodara was the chief, the others being Trypimeni, Antiphoniti, Agia Marina, and Agios Nicola. The fief passed out of their hands on the Turkish conquest of the island in 1570.

Meanwhile, Rizo-Karpaso had obtained the doubtful distinction of becoming the residence of the Greek bishop of Famagusta; this anomalous arrangement was the result of the Concordia[1], brought about at Famagusta in 1222 by the legate Pelagius, sent expressly to Cyprus to settle the difficult questions which had arisen during the last thirty years from the simultaneous presence of bishops and clergy of both the Western and Eastern churches. It was probably to minimise the chance of further collisions that Pelagius, while sanctioning the presence of four Orthodox bishops for the future, contrived that each should take up his residence as far as possible from the old see, and, indeed, from the centres of civilisation. Thus were banished —the bishop of Nicosia to the Solia valley in the Forest Range, a long day's journey from his metropolis; the bishop of Paphos to Arsos in the recesses of the western hills; the bishop of Limassol to Lefkara among the foothills of Machaeras; and the bishop of Famagusta to the extreme eastern end of the island, where thirty miles up the peninsula lies Rizo-Karpaso. Needless to say, the Orthodox bishops were not satisfied with these arrangements, and 250 years later Pope Sixtus IV, on hearing of continual offences against the Concordia, despatched a Bull[2], once more defining the bounds which must not be exceeded.

That the Carpass was entirely unmolested by the Turks is disproved by the existence of so many ruined churches in its area, and of Greek-speaking Mahometan villages like Galinoporni and Korovia, sure traces of a forced conversion of the conquered. But mixed villages are rare, and the Christian community seems to have held its own and to have slipped less into the slough than elsewhere in Cyprus. Under the Turkish, as now under the English, rule it remained under the jurisdiction of Famagusta, and it is certainly better developed at present than any other remote district of the island.

The Carpass has not been often visited by archaeologists since the Ottoman rule was established in Cyprus; the best description of its antiquities is that of Pococke, published in 1745 (vol. ii.

[1] The text is given in Mas Latrie, vol. iii. p. 622.

[2] Ibid p. 315.

3. 3), but that most admirable of explorers is all too brief, and although in successive excursions from Gialousa he saw almost everything worth seeing in the district he contents himself with little more than a mere enumeration of the ancient remains. Second to this comes the account of Sakellarios (*Κυπριακά*, i. chaps. 11, 12, 13). Sibthorpe, Leake, Von Hammer, and Ross[1] saw various districts of the island but not the Carpass: M. Waddington, like most travellers, did not go beyond Salamis (Voy. Arch. iii): General di Cesnola implies in his map of 'Travels and Explorations' that he had seen the Carpass pretty thoroughly, but his letterpress shows a very imperfect acquaintance with it, while his brother's excursions therein resulted in no gain to science (Salaminia, Introduction). M. de la Mas Latrie explored the base of the peninsula but did not penetrate to Rizo-Karpaso (Bibl. de l'École des Chartes, xli. p. 375). Von Löher was never in the Carpass at all (Reiseberichte in d. Insel Cypern 1878), nor could he be reckoned an archaeological traveller; the latter remark applies also to Sir Samuel Baker ('Cyprus as I saw it in 1879'), and Mrs. Scott-Stevenson ('Our home in Cyprus'); the former gives an excellent geological and topographical account of the peninsula, but ignores its antiquities; the latter was only three and a half days in the Carpass.

I determined therefore as early as January to examine systematically the ancient remains of this district, as soon as I should be able to leave Papho. Accordingly in July, after spending a few days in and about Famagusta and Salamis, I travelled into the peninsula, and visited every village except Komi Kebir, Galatia, and the small hamlets at the base, which Dr. Guillemard had examined earlier in the year: and in describing the district, I propose to proceed in geographical order along the southern coast to Cape St. Andréas and back by the northern to the territory of Kyrenia.

*Salamis.* Before entering the Carpass a few words should be said upon the ruins of the ancient capital at the mouth of the Pediaeus—ruins to which no others in Cyprus are comparable for extent and variety. They and their history have been too often described[2] for me to enter into detail. I regarded them mainly

[1] Dr. Sibthorpe, who travelled in 1787, turned north-westward from Salamis, (Walpole's Travels in Turkey, ii. pp. 17 foll.). Col. Leake merely passed across the island from Kyrenia to Larnaca and v.v. in 1800 (Walpole, ii. pp. 243 foll.). Ross in 1845 saw Kantara Castle, but did not proceed east (Reise auf Kos und Cypern, p. 134).

[2] Pococke, vol. ii. pp. 214 foll.; A. Cesnola, 'Salaminia,' Introd.; M. O. Richter in Journal of Hell. Studies, vol. iv. pp. 112 foll.; A. H. Sayce in a letter to the 'Academy,' March 1888; and others.

from the point of view of the excavator, and after remarking that the large building in the western centre of the site, known to the villagers as the *Λουτρόν*, appears to me to be not mediaeval, as has been suggested, but of late Roman or Byzantine work, and to have been a receptacle wherein the water brought in by the aqueduct, whose broken arches still remain, might be stored and cooled, I will proceed to the consideration of future researches. The whole seaward side of the site is a succession of hillocks, clogged with drifted sand, which at the northern end has raised all to a common level, while upon the south is a marsh formed by those deposits of the Pediaeus which have silted up the harbour, and left faint traces only of its quays and piers above ground. In all this tract there is of course no indication as to what lies buried beneath, and the digger must run exploratory trenches in all directions before fixing on a spot for his work; but considering the evident depth of deposit, the rapidity with which archaeological treasures were probably hidden from rapacious eyes by the sand, and the fact that, whenever the peasants of Enkomi or Agios Sergios filch a corner of land from the Crown and proceed to plough it, they find gems, coins and small antiques in greater abundance than on any other site in the island (over a dozen gems, recently so found, were shown to me in Limnia and Agios Sergios), I cannot but hope that some attempt will be made to cut into the sand-hills and the marsh.

On the landward side is a hideous chaos of stone, squared and unsquared, marble and granite shafts, fragments of cornices and capitals, but hardly a clear trace of any one building. There are, however, two places in this wilderness where I longed to set a few diggers to work; the one is near the south-western corner of the site, just within the walls, where a fluted shaft of white marble, evidently deeply buried, is peeping out of the ground; the other is at the north-western angle beyond the *Λουτρόν* where in a well-defined oblong depression, much choked with sand, lie half-buried a number of glistening granite shafts of very large diameter—quite half as large again as any on the site of New Paphos: the sand here is strewn with fragments of a white marble pavement. That this is a temple-site I have little doubt, deeply buried enough to make the chance of finding treasures fairly good. Professor Sayce was perfectly right in describing[1] all that is now above

[1] In his 'Academy' letter, *v. supra.*

ground here, as at New Paphos and Soli, as of a late period, and it cannot but be admitted that our failure to find an earlier layer beneath the existing ruins of the temple of Aphrodite at Old Paphos, is not encouraging: but I submit that the chances at Salamis are better: for here we have a very ancient city of much greater size than any other in the island, which has been twice destroyed[1] and rebuilt on its own ruins, and upon which, whether from river deposits or sand, silt has accumulated with great rapidity. It was adorned by one temple of great antiquity and renown,—that of Zeus Salaminius—compared by Ammianus Marcellinus[2] to the great shrine at Paphos; by that of Athena Pronoea, also of note[3]; besides lesser shrines[4] in which, as in that of Zeus, Asiatic rites and human sacrifice were practised. Further, the cemeteries which surround the city are very far from being exhausted; where Alexander di Cesnola was working when the British Government stopped him in 1879, and where the peasants still open graves from time to time, there is a very good season's work yet to be done.

*Enkomi.* In the neighbouring village of Enkomi I saw a headless stone lion, said to have been found in a large tomb about a year ago. He sits on his haunches in a stiff attitude, and is three feet high: the execution is archaic but bold, and he has evidently guarded one of the sides of an entrance. The tomb is said to have been filled up again, and it probably contains the fellow.

A small fragment of granite had been picked up on the site a day or two before my arrival, bearing the following inscription in small and good lettering. It is broken on all sides:

| 12. | \ЄΙΜυ | . . . . . . . . . . . |
|---|---|---|
| | ΔΙΑΤЄΤΑ | . . . *διατετα[γμένον* . . |
| | ꓘΝΚΑΙϹΑ | . . . . *Καίσα[ρα* . . |
| | ΙΙΛΥΤϹ | . . . . . . . . . . . . . |
| | Η ΡϹ\ | . . . . . . . . . . . |

Probably a fragment of a honorific inscription commemorating the despatch of some Salaminian on a *πρεσβεία* to the Emperor.

*Limnia.* In the surrounding villages, so often visited, I hardly expected to find any unpublished inscriptions: but nevertheless in

[1] Once by the Jews in the time of Trajan; and once by the great earthquake which occurred in the reign of Constantine, after which it was rebuilt as Constantia.

[2] xiv. 14. Cf. also Tac. Ann. iii. 62; Lactantius, i. 21.

[3] Ovid, Metam. xiv. 759 foll.

[4] Porphyr. de Abstinentia, ii. 54.

Limnia, about half an hour's ride to the north-west, I copied five, which are certainly not in any publication with which I am acquainted, besides others already correctly published.

13. A stone fragment in the yard of Hadji Anastasi Panagi :

ᴗ///ΝΤΙ/ . . . . . _ΥΝΙΕΝΗ
. . . . . . [σ]υν[γ]ενῆ

a title of honour at the Ptolemaic court. Cf. Inscriptions of Paphos, etc. *passim.*

14. Ibid. fragment of a blue limestone pedestal, built into the wall of Dimitri H. Giorgi.

Fair lettering 1½ in. long. Broken top and right, and much worn on the surface.

| | |
|---|---|
| ᴗ Ι | . . . . . |
| Α \ Κ Ο | . . . . . |
| Σ Υ Γ Γ Ε Ν Η Ι | *συγγενῆ* |
| Τ Η Σ Π Ο Λ Ε | *τῆς πόλε[ως.* |

15. Ibid. in the wall of the house of the same Dimitri ; a block of stone, with letters 1½ in. long :

| | |
|---|---|
| ΣΕΙ ΟΥΙΟΝΣΟΥΛΠΙΚΙΟΝ | *Σερούιον Σουλπίκιον* |
| ΠΑΓΚΛΕΑΟΥΗΡΑΝΙΑΝΟΝ | *Παγκλέα Οὐηρανιανὸν* |
| ΟΝΗΣΑΝΔΡΟΣΑΞ/// ΑΒΑΤΟΥ | *'Ονήσανδρος 'Αξ[ι]αβάτου ?* |
| ΚΑΤΑΔΙΑΘΗΚΗΝ | *κατὰ διαθήκην.* |

Cf. an inscription relating to the same individual published in Lebas and Waddington, vol. iii. No. 2759.

16. Pedestal of blue limestone ibid., built into Maria Manjalou's wall. Coarse letters 1½ in. long, and difficult to read.

| | |
|---|---|
| ΧΡΕΟΦΥΛΑΞΙΙΙ | *Χρεοφύλαξι(ν)* |
| ΦΙΛΤΩΝΟΠΡΟΣΤΗΙΔΙ///// \Ο////// | *Φίλτων ὁ πρὸς τῇ δι[α]λο[γῇ* |
| ΤΩΝΕΝΤΩΙΧΡΕ/// ΦΥΛΑΚΙ ///. Ι | *τῶν ἐν τῷ χρε[ο]φυλακί[ῳ* |
| ΒΥΒΛΙΟ ///ΚΑΙΚΙ //·//// ΑΣ | *βυβλίω[ν] καὶ Κί[νν]ας* |
| ΑΡΕΣΤΟΥΓΡΑΜ /////// ΕΥΩΝ | *'Αρέστου γραμ[ματ]εύων* |
| CΛΒL | *σλβ' L.* • |

*Χρεοφυλάκιον* = the archives where lists of public debtors were kept, cf. C. I. G. 2826, 38; it is known only from inscriptions, and therefore *χρεοφύλαξ*, though a hitherto unknown word, need not be questioned: *διαλογή* must mean 'sorting' or 'arranging': Philto's office amounted to that of a book-keeper; and he with the clerk, Cinna, dedicates to the heads of the department. The date, if reckoned from the era of the province, is A. D. 174.

17. Ibid. on a large block of stone in the village street, worn nearly smooth, and broken on all sides.

ΙϹΤΟΝ

ΤΟΝ.

These inscriptions were all shown to me by the village school-master, a Gialousa man of considerable intelligence, who stated that a stranger had copied some of them a few years before, 'but he did not seem to be much of an *ἀρχαιολόγος*.' He guided me also to a house, in whose courtyard lay a very florid Ionic capital of coarse pink marble, one and a half feet in diameter, and a portion of a Roman oil-mill of black basalt [1]. Built into the porch of the next house was a fragment of a coarse frieze, representing birds and dogs, but frightfully defaced. In many walls in Limnia may be seen fragments of florid Byzantine mouldings, relics of the former church of Agia Sophia; and the villagers possess many gems, coins, and small antiquities, collected from the site of Salamis; I bought four intaglios of no particular interest—the best representing Eros *τοξοφόρος*. In

*Agios Sergios.* Agios Sergios I found two more intaglios, but no other relics of antiquity worth recording, while in Alodá survives

*Alodá.* only the usual tale of a written stone, long ago carried off to

*Spathariko* Trikomo. In Spathariko, formerly an Armenian village, to the north of Salamis, are many Roman rock tombs, in which the villagers say that gold ornaments and glass have been found. This was the hottest spot I ever found in Cyprus, and one of the poorest and filthiest: such hospitality as they could show the villagers readily offered, but the heat reflected from the naked rock, and the pitiless scirocco combined with the effects of a bad fall the day before, which had skinned my face and hands, to give me an evil recollection of my last halting-place in the Mesaoréa.

*The Vallia.* Late in the afternoon we set out for the Carpass itself, and leaving the plain rode along the sea-shore, crossing many

[1] Vid. *supra*, p. 28.

torrent-beds which came down from among the foot-hills of the Northern Range. At a point below Monargá, where the road can barely pass between cliff and sea, I was told that some rough statuettes had been found by the road-makers. After this defile the hills recede and leave a fertile plain, on the further side of which lies the prosperous mixed village of Gastriá under the cliffs of the Vallia. *Gastriá.*

While resting in the coffee-house here an inscribed stele was brought to me which had been found in the Vallia; it had a low pediment, and (as Prof. W. M. Ramsay suggested to me) appears, from the employment in two cases out of three of O for OY, to belong to the fourth century. It read thus:

18. ΣΥΜΜΑΧΟΕΣΤΙΤ
ΟΣΑΜΑΤΡΙΗΡΑΡΧΟ
ΚΝΙΔΙΟΥ

Συμμάχο(υ) ἐστι τὸ σᾶμα τριηράρχο(υ) Κνιδίου.

This seems to be a rude attempt at a spondaic hexameter. *Akrotiri.* The stele was said to have been found in the Vallia among Cnidus. the extensive ruins which I visited next day, and of which the only extant description is that of Sakellarios[1]. They are known as Akrotiri, and lie on the extreme southern point—the Cape Elaea of Ptolemy; and this Gastriá inscription is of some topographical importance if it identifies them with those of the lost Cyprian Cnidus[2], the birthplace of the historian Ctesias, according to Tzetzes:

Ὁ δὲ Κτησίας ἰατρὸς, υἱὸς τοῦ Κτησιόχου
Ἐξωρμημένος πόλεως ἐκ Κνίδου τῆς Κυπρίας[3].

Suidas (s. v. *Κτησίας*) calls him a Cnidian without specifying to which town of that name he belonged; and the only other probable reference to this Cnidus seems to be made by Ovid (Metamorph. x. 530), who ranks it with the great shrines of Aphrodite in Cyprus:

'Non alto repetit Paphon aequore cinctam,
Piscosamque Cnidon, gravidamque Amathunta metallis[4]'.

Curiously enough, Sakellarios'[5] identified it with Koma tou

[1] Κυπριακά, vol. i. p. 155. Dr. Guillemard had made a careful examination of them earlier in the year.

[2] Engel, Kypros, vol. i. p. 157.

[3] Chiliad. i. 83.

[4] But it may be intended in many passages, usually understood of the Carian Cnidus; e. g. Horace, Odes, i. 30.

[5] p. 154.

Gialou, a few miles only to the east, on the very slender evidence of this word *piscosa*: finding Byzantine remains (all quite late and unimportant) in Koma and learning that the natives lived mainly by fishing, he jumped to a conclusion which narrowly missed being right. Akrotiri he identified with another lost city, Acra (Steph. Byz. s.v.); but ἀκροτήριον is too common a designation for a modern headland to be readily accepted as a survival of any name of antiquity.

I have little to add to Sakellarios' description of the principal site—indeed I saw less than he did, for I failed, whether from the denseness of the undergrowth or of my perception, to discern the 'gates of the city,' or any 'colossal pillars.' To my eyes it was a wilderness of formless heaps, extending round a small bay for about half-a-mile, and inland for some four hundred yards. Large 'oil-stones' are seen here and there (the cape was called Ἐλαῖα), and many traces of houses and city wall, but no temple or very large building. The rock is everywhere too near the surface to make excavation profitable, and only the tombs would repay exploration. I heard that Alexander di Cesnola's diggers opened five or six, and that Mr. Hamilton Lang had also caused the site to be tried. In a large open tomb, approached by a rock staircase, I found fragments of early buff and red unglazed pottery of the 'Paraskeve' class, and the circular form of the chambers indicated a fairly early date[1]. In another which was blocked up, my guide (an old tomb-robber from Agios Theodoros) informed me that there were 'forty columns': if this is more than the usual romance, it may mean either that the tomb has a façade with two or three pillars like those at New Paphos[2] and Phlamoudhi[3], or (more probably) that it contains several cippi, so often found in late graves.

But the most interesting feature lies about one hundred and fifty yards to the east, and a like distance from the sea—a stone enclosure[4], represented in the annexed illustration, a reproduction of a photograph taken by Dr. Guillemard.

The enclosure is rectangular and oblong, the long sides lying nearly true east and west, and measuring 37 ft. from the outer faces of the walls: the short sides are 21 ft. 5 in. in length, similarly measured. The stones average about

[1] See the article on Tombs in the Journal of Hell. Studies, vol. ix.

[2] Cesnola, Cyprus, p. 224.

[3] Vid. *infra*, p. 98.

[4] Sakellarios cannot have seen this, for he makes no mention of it.

*To face p. 66.*

*Collotype.* *Oxford University Press.*

STONE-ENCLOSURE AT AKROTIRI IN THE VALLIA.

FROM A PHOTOGRAPH BY DR. F. H. H. GUILLEMARD.

1 ft. in thickness, rise 2 ft. above the ground, and range from 6 to 2 ft. in length. They stand in close contact with each other. The north-west angle is composed of a great upright block, obviously a menhir or an emblem of fertility; its full height from the ground is 6 ft. 9 in., and its width and thickness each 2 ft. 10 in. It tapers slightly, but is not pierced, though a slight incision has been made, apparently by chance, in one side. I have no doubt that the enclosure has never been higher, nor is it silted up, for some disappointed treasure-seeker has revealed the rock a few inches below the surface. The blocks, which are of the common limestone of the district, have been shaped and roughly dressed, and all are much worn, but some bore traces of a chisel-draft round the inner face, the centre of the stone being thus raised in relief,—no uncommon characteristic of Phoenician work [1].

That this is a Phoenician relic there can be little question; stone enclosures with upright menhirs are frequent on the opposite coasts [2], although the usual form is circular. Major Conder, R.E. [3], quotes an example of a quadrangle at 'Adlun between Sidon and Tyre, the long sides containing six, the short, two stones apiece. Here however the blocks are not contiguous as in the Cyprian instance. It should be noticed that where in England a single menhir stands in a circle, it is usually upon the north-east, and is supposed to stand in relation to the rising of the sun at the summer solstice; in the present case, if the relation be solar at all, the setting sun must be indicated, as it disappears behind the rock of Kantara, the most conspicuous object in the landscape. It must be added that there is and can be no trace of sepulture either in or near the enclosure, the solid rock cropping out in all directions; and this singular example of a large class of stone monuments must depend for its explanation on that assigned to its fellows all over the world.

*Camaraes.*

In juxtaposition to this Phoenician monument should be placed the three monoliths which stand over tomb-doors at Camaraes or Tria Litharia, on the eastern edge of the Vallia, about an hour's ride from Akrotiri; and we will pass rapidly by the stone-heaps at Agia Thora, which probably represent a suburban dependency of Cnidus, and by a spot known as Pallura in the centre of the forest, where some fragments of

[1] But cf. *supra*, p. 5.

[2] See Conder, Syrian Stone Lore, pp. 43 foll.

[3] Heth and Moab, p. 237. Cf. also p 243.

rough stone statuary of the conventional early Cyprian type were lying on the rock.

The tombs at Camaraes are three in number, approached by δρόμοι nearly six feet wide (a sign of antiquity in Cyprus), and now rifled and empty. They face east, looking from the cliff of the Vallia on to the plain of Vokolidha, and on the surface of the ground under which the tomb-doors are cut stood (for one only is still upright) three roughly shaped monoliths, the height of a man, two feet and a-half broad by one thick, tapering and rounded at the top. Like the menhir at Akrotiri, the guardians of these three lonely tombs have no mark of any kind upon them [1].

*Agios Theodoros.*

The large village of Agios Theodoros, which lies behind low hills bounding the forest tract of the Vallia, has no antiquities more interesting than a Roman milestone, already published.

*Koma tou Gialou.*

Neither Vokolidha nor Tavros have anything to show, and we follow the road to Koma tou Gialou—'the village of the beach' (αἰγιαλοῦ)—one of the prettiest and richest in the Carpass, and identified by Sakellarios, for the insufficient reasons stated above, with 'piscosa Cnidus.' Byzantine remains there are undoubtedly, and the native imagination runs riot as usual over the number of churches Koma once possessed: certainly some remains of four are still standing, and seven more sites are pointed out. In the ruins of that of the Panagia I found two fragments of limestone cornice which proved to fit on to each other, and to bear parts of one inscription. The lettering was about 1½ in. long and of late period; the middle hopelessly gone.

19. //ΛΛΛΙCΤΩΚΟ /// Ν ////////////////// ΙΗΝΑΛΟΧΟ ///

*Κ]αλλιστῷ Κο[ί]ν[τος . . . . . . . . .] τὴν ἄλοχο[ν.*

It is not improbable that here, as at Letymbou in the Papho district and in other Cypriote villages where the number of churches is out of all proportion to the population, some of the ruins are those of Latin edifices. Koma tou Gialou may well have attracted Venetian settlers to its little bay sheltered by a headland on the east and by the Vallia on the west, and to its fertile, well-watered plain: and my supposition was curiously

[1] Most unfortunately my photograph was a failure.

illustrated a little later; for while I was resting in one of the coffee-houses of the village a peasant reported a cave with a written rock above it, lying to the east: he offered himself as guide, and led us half an hour's journey to a spot near the sea-shore, where by a little ruined church dedicated to St. Anna was a quarry, and on its face the date

M̊DXXXIII.

proving that the quarry was worked about forty years before the loss of Cyprus by Venice, and perhaps furnished stone for the building of churches at Koma tou Gialou.

From this point to Cape St. Andréas the southern slopes of the Carpass become more and more wild; the villages, with the exception of Neta, retire from the sea, and before them lies a craggy ridge of almost virgin forest, traversed only by a few rough paths, and stretching down to the shore: few human habitations appear for many miles, and, if any there be, they are mere summer-huts, deserted except during the reaping of the little tracts reclaimed here and there from the wilderness. But the evidences of ancient inhabitation are not infrequent; no less than three sites are to be seen, choked with undergrowth and hemmed in by the impenetrable 'schinia' shrubs, in the tract lying between Leonarisso and the sea. The largest—now known as Mazaraes and not marked on the Inch Survey—lies on the top of the first rocky ridge in a strong position above a second site, marked on the map as Kakozonara, which, being very small and unimportant, is probably that of an outlying village built about a well.

*Mazaraes, Kakozonara, and Katsari.*

Of 'Mazaraes,' in spite of its large area of ruin—nearly half a mile square—there is hardly anything to determine the character or date. Like a score of forgotten sites in Cyprus it is a wilderness of grey stone, of which half is unsquared, with here and there a patch of clearing from whose surface the peasants have removed and heaped up the débris. No mouldings, no architectural details could I discover—only a few oil-stones, and some blocks of unusual size piled together in one heap; and no better evidence was forthcoming than that of a dozen rifled rock tombs which lie near the southern centre of the site. Argument drawn from such insufficient data as the width of a δρόμος or the shape of sepulchral chambers is never convincing; but so far as it is worth anything, it would suggest an early date for the town to which these tombs belonged: the δρόμοι are wide and the chambers in some instances circular, like those in the fourth century group known as 'Ἀλώνια τοῦ Ἐπισκόπου near New Paphos; and other negative evidence may be quoted to support this inference. Were it a Byzantine ruin, experience of Cyprus would lead one to expect the remains of one or more churches and almost invariably a tradition of sanctity attaching to a ruined apse with a rough pile of stones in the centre representing the former altar: a Ptolemaic or Roman town would have probably survived into Byzantine times and have left evidence of itself in the shape of concrete pavements and florid mouldings; and I am inclined therefore to refer this site to earlier days, perhaps to the sixth or fifth century before our era; the very absence of all architectural features among ruins whose blocks are so large affords in itself a presumption of antiquity. The rough and unglazed potsherds, which were all that I could pick up upon the site, might have been of any period.

A place of some strength it must have been, for a cliff breaks away below it on all sides but the north; and on the sea-shore half a mile to the south-east I found traces of what was perhaps its 'scala,' a little patch of the usual grey ruin, now known as Katzari, strewn with rough red potsherds, and here and there large squared blocks among rubble. Deep down into the limestone rock has been bored a well-shaft, and there are faint traces of a considerable building, perhaps a tower, on a little rising ground overlooking the tiny bay.

The name and history of this forgotten town are probably for ever lost; and I can hazard no conjecture, except that 'Mazaraes' possibly contains the name Makar (in Cypriote pronunciation 'Madjar'), and is a survival of a Phoenician settlement.

A deep valley intervenes before the central ridge of the Carpass, on which due north of Mazaraes lies the long village of Leonarisso, where I camped for two nights, and was tormented by clouds of insects brought up by the hot wind[1]. On the very crest of the ridge, about half an hour to the N.N.W., *Peristefáni.* I was shown a curious site, where a 'stranger' was said to have dug a few years before: it is now known as Peristefani, and covers a small area only, but is remarkable both for its remains and for the extraordinary strength of its position; except from

[1] The heat for the last week had been so terribly aggravated by the scirocco that the melons, figs, and vines had been ruined, the wells were drying up, and a woman fell dead of sunstroke on a threshing-floor at Leonarisso the day that I arrived. To this is due the failure of almost all my subsequent photographs, for my whole stock of films was so much spoilt, that no decent print could be taken from them.

the south-east this peninsula of crag is perfectly inaccessible. Thé peasants have brought the little plateau under cultivation, and collected the surface-ruin into heaps, or built it into fences, obliterating all traces of foundations; but here and there from fence or heap project the torsos or legs of large stone statues of a very early period, the most remarkable of which I gathered together and photographed:—

(1) A female figure, nude; head and legs below the knee broken off. When complete it must have stood about nine feet high. Arms close to the side and hardly distinguishable from the trunk; similarly the legs are hardly divided, and the back is flat and unworked.

(2) A female head, found separate but possibly belonging to the above, measuring sixteen inches from the point of the chin to the crown. The face is much mutilated. The hair falls straight to the nape of the neck and then curls upwards, but is not worked in detail.

(3) Shoulders and lower half of the head of a male figure, nude. Most noticeable is the wedge-shaped beard, not worked in detail. This figure again must have been much over life-size.

(4) A draped torso, about the size of life, apparently female, and having the right hand upon the breasts; probably a representation of the Asiatic Goddess?

The sculptures give the spectator a strong impression of antiquity; the stiff pose and rude style recalling the more archaic Dali figurines.

I picked up also, besides much rough pottery, two of those prehistoric' stones, flattened on one side and rounded on the other, which have been found on many early sites in Cyprus, and are supposed to have been used for purposes of crushing grain [1]. Any foundations that ever existed on the centre of the plateau have been obliterated, and no traces exist in the rock round the edges to suggest that there was ever any wall or fortress; it seems therefore most probable that these statues are the relics of a solitary temple, possibly of the Asiatic Goddess, which looked down from the crest of the Carpass on to both seas, and across to the Cilician coast whence she came.

*Lythrankomi.*

To complete the survey of this group of ancient sites we must pass eastward from Leonarisso, through Vasili, to Lythrankomi, where the ground east of the village shows traces of a former settlement. Close to the small monastery of the Panagia tou

[1] See Journal of Hell. Studies, vol. ix. p. 154.

Lythrankomou are three large blocks about three feet by two, set on edge, one having a deep depression in its upper surface; but it would be rash to assert that they belong to any such sacred enclosure as we have seen at Akrotiri, although it is not impossible.

When, after passing through Vathylakka and Agios Symeon—the latter being the first of a line of four Moslem villages—we next meet with ancient remains, they are of a remarkable order. The ridge of the Carpass has now become higher, and the whole aspect of the country more rugged and mountainous; deep gorges run down from the backbone to the sea, and precipitous flat-topped hills become a feature in the landscape. It is while passing under one such hill, after abruptly descending from the central ridge and within sight of Elisis, that the traveller suddenly perceives high up in the cliff upon his right a dark patch, which a moment's scrutiny convinces him must be the mouth of an artificial cave[1]. If he turns off his path, as we did on that blazing midday in July, and, tethering his horse at the foot of the hill, bursts his way for five hundred feet of ascent through matted thorns and over rocks so hot as to blister the bare hand, until he reaches the foot of the scarp which forms the crest of the hill, he will have had no bad foretaste of purgatory. And still the door of the cave—now evidently artificial—is fully twenty feet above his head. The rock is sheer and even slightly overhanging, and for a few minutes he will see no way up its smooth face; but a long ledge in the cliff face, running obliquely across it and passing under the cave-door, ends in a turn of the cliff about fifteen feet above the ground, and careful search will reveal the possibility of reaching it by means of knobs and cracks on the face of the precipice; and, once therein, it is fairly easy, though most unpleasant, to wriggle the body along the ledge, which is not more than a foot wide, until immediately under the opening, and get into the latter with a sigh of relief, tempered by the consciousness of having to descend that sloping ledge again sooner or later. But, standing upright in the doorway, the climber will not regret his labour, for the largest of ancient Cyprian sepulchres lies before him.

*Cave at Elisis.*

The plan below shows the arrangement of the aisles and niches, but its measurements are not quite accurate, as I had no tape, and had to measure by paces.

[1] Pococke (p. 220) saw this cave, which he calls Agi Mama, but he seems to have failed to get into it. Sakellarios (p. 153) heard of it, but somehow did not see it. Mrs. Scott-Stevenson saw it, but rode on.

It will be seen that this tomb is cut for 87 feet straight into the precipice. 12 feet is taken up by the passage which runs down to the door, and then the great hall opens out divided into a central nave, supported on four arches, and flanked on each side by aisles, from the farther sides of which run out the sepulchral chambers, four on the

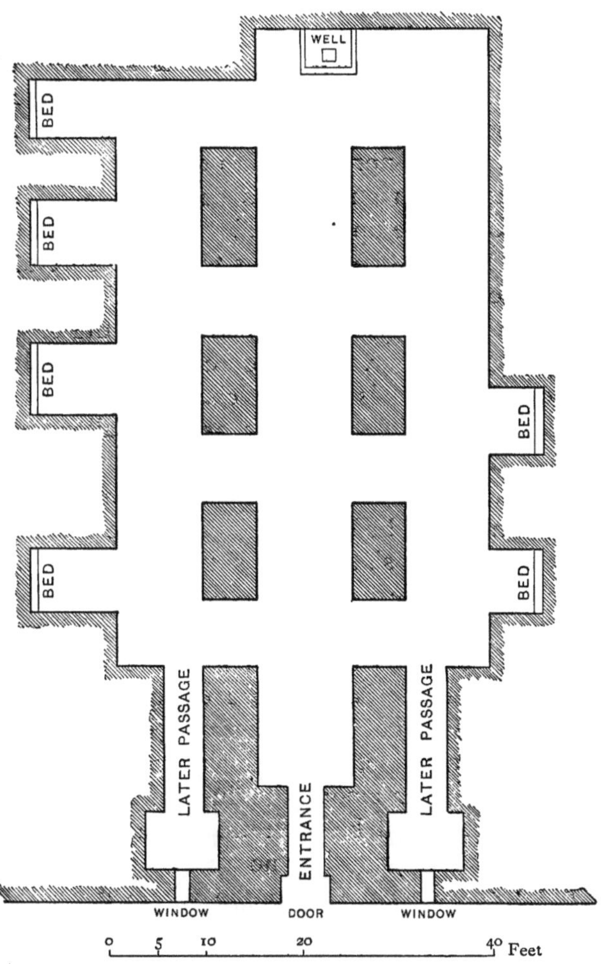


left and two more shallow on the right, the tomb never having been completely finished on the first plan. The whole is rather flatly vaulted, and not more than seven feet high; the floor is perfectly even, and covered with a couple of inches of coarse dust, the detritus of the roof; the cutting is in all parts regular and careful. On either hand of the entrance runs a narrow passage, opening out into a little chamber, which is lighted by a slit in the face of the cliff: these may be relics of a time when the cave was used as a refuge or a stronghold, and seem to be of later period than the rest. The peasants of Elisis have a tradition that robbers once used it, and the roof is in places blackened by smoke, while cinders and dung are to be seen on the floor. The beds in the sepulchral niches lie across the inner end, in shallow recesses. At the far end of the Tomb is a square arched recess containing what is apparently a well, cut perhaps in later times, and a stone which I threw down seemed to bound and rebound from its sides to infinity; but I had neither the means nor the will to descend the shaft, more especially as persuasion and threats had alike failed to induce my servant to follow me up the cliff. In no part of the tomb —and I looked most diligently—was there any sort of inscription, excepting only two or three names of modern Greeks who had climbed up in past years, and had carved the sides of the entrance after their manner. The whole cave is absolutely empty[1].

At the foot of the cliff is a small chamber, probably a tomb, running some six feet into the rock, and a shallow depression to the right of it—both empty.

Such is the most remarkable of Cyprian tombs, whether for size or situation[2]: but before considering the question of its character and date, the similar (but smaller) example at Galinóporni, three miles to the east, must be described[3].

*Cave at Galinóporni.*

It is cut in the face of a precipitous hill, which looks S.E., immediately east of the village and near the well and ruined church of St. Anna. It is far more easily accessible, and, a false door having been cut on the left of the true entrance, has been long used as a stable, a fact which accounts for the goats' bones lying on the floor among the dust (in this instance often two feet deep). As will be seen from the plan, it is a few feet shorter (68 ft. 8 in.) and has no aisles, only deep chambers running out from the nave. On the whole it has the same general characteristics, but is slightly more lofty—nine feet at the highest point; the cutting is hardly so careful; the first

[1] The plan bears a striking resemblance to one published by M. Rénan (Mission en Phénicie, p. 869) of a tomb at Mogharet-es-Souk, but of the date of the latter there is no direct evidence given.

[2] I tried to photograph the scarp from the slope below, but could get no effective view; and the heat reflected from the rock was so tremendous, and our thirst so great, that I hurried back to the horses: in the two or three minutes that my camera stood in the sun the brass-work became too hot to touch.

[3] Sir S. Baker was taken to this cave (p. 121).

chamber on the left has a square recess in its side wall; and there are three square holes in the floor in different parts of the tomb, filled up with stones. The villagers have grubbed among the dust for treasure, but found none.

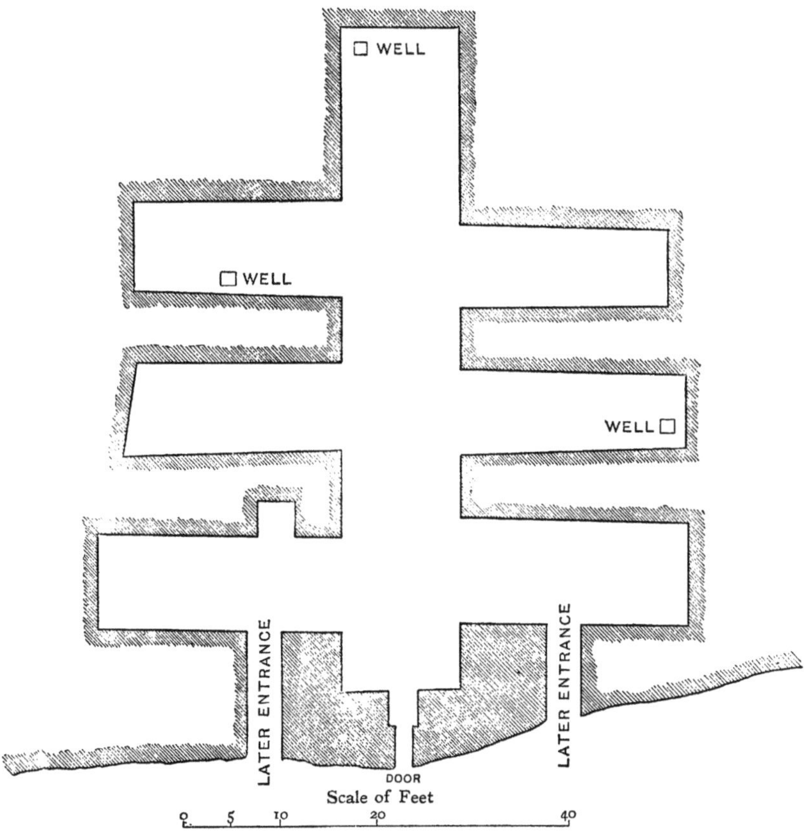


Why then were these great caves cut out of the rock, who cut them, and when? The answer to the first question is not doubtful. Tombs they were in the first instance beyond all question; the niches and beds establish this at once: and we may safely conjecture that they were the burying-places of great families. The latter points however are not so readily settled: there is little 'internal' evidence to guide us: the arching and vaulting might belong to any period but the latest; no stalactite has formed whereby we might estimate the centuries that have passed since water first dripped in these dark abodes of the dead; the cutting has been done with an adze-like tool—about an inch broad in the blade—but so has that of most Cyprian tombs; and we must appeal to any other remains which seem to be of the same period and afford better indications.

The great tomb at Elisis stands alone, no smaller graves are hollowed out beside it as by the royal sepulchres of Phrygia, and no ancient site can be detected for some miles round; but at Galinóporni a hundred other rock-cut graves honeycomb the eastern slope on which the village is built: the houses are often built on to them, and they are used as inner rooms, as store-chambers, as stables—indeed the natives are half troglodyte. Many of these tombs are square pits sunk into a flat plateau of rock, and would therefore have been open to the sky had they not been covered with a lid of some kind; the ledges on which this lid rested are seen an inch or two below the top of the tomb walls[1]. Now this characteristic is, I believe, very rare in Cyprus: in a group of tombs known as 'Ελληνικά, near New Paphos, and bearing Cypriote inscriptions, I have noticed it[2]; and in the necropolis of Macaria (vid. *infra*, p. 103) a few tombs occur, sunk in the solid rock and covered by ordinary sarcophagus-lids, in this case however not resting on a ledge, but on the top of the rock itself. I know of no other instances, but M. Rénan (Mission en Phénicie, pp. 225, 229, 288, etc., and Plate XXXI) remarked it frequently on the opposite coast at Gharfin, Maschnaka, and other places in the districts of Tyre and Byblos. The general plan of the Galinóporni tomb should be compared with that of one at Sidon on p. 437 of M. Rénan's book. It seems therefore clear that this fashion of sepulture was introduced into Cyprus from Phoenicia; and as we find no other instance of its prevalence except this at Galinóporni, we may conclude that the graves at the latter are of about the same period as those at New Paphos (fifth or fourth century?), and are perhaps Phoenician.

But where is the city to which these graves belonged? I confess that I can give only a tentative answer. Pococke states that he saw 'some small ruins of an antient place which might be Urania' on a hill above Galinóporni: if he was right, I failed to find them, and in any case they are probably not those of Urania, which seem to be situated at Aphendrika. Failing these ruins—of whose existence I am sceptical, for I

[1] This peculiarity was also noticed here by Pococke, who had previously remarked it on the site upon Cape Dinaretum; vid. *infra*.

[2] See article on 'Tombs' in Journ. Hellen. Studies, vol. ix, and 'Sammlung,' No. 33.

questioned the villagers most closely, and they showed every inclination to guide me to all ancient sites that they knew of with a view to attracting our money to their neighbourhood in another season[1]—I can only refer both the Elisis and the Galinóporni tombs to a large site which lies on the coast at a point due south of Korovia; as the crow flies it is distant two and a-half miles from the Elisis cave, and a little more than three from Galinóporni.

*Agia Varvára.*

The ruins extend for half a mile westward of the ruined church of Agia Varvára (miscalled Agios Giorgios in the Survey), and cover the slope inland for some three hundred yards. At the western extremity, overlooking the sea, is a knoll which appears to have been the citadel: a low cliff falls to the beach, and inland another cliff walls in the site. Here, as at Mazaraes, search as I might, I could find neither columns nor mouldings of any description: only very large blocks of stone, a carefully built water channel, some large 'oil-stones,' and rough red pottery. The church has a double apse, and seems to have been built from the débris of the town: were it in any way connected with the latter in point of date, we should have expected to find remains of other churches in so large a ruin. I could see no trace of any harbour.

Such an entire absence of architectural features might equally argue an early site, or a ruined modern village: the size of the building material is against the latter alternative, but, if it were not for a stone head now in a house at Korovia and affirmed on all hands to have been found at Agia Varvára, certainty would have been impossible. This head however, of which I append a wood-cut taken from a photograph, is clearly not a product of modern Cyprus: it is life-size, the moustache and short curling beard are treated in detail, and the eye-sockets are

[1] It is true that a certain Mustapha some years ago found a pit in his garden at Galinóporni from which he obtained some stone heads, now built into his gate, and some fragments of statuary now in his garden. He averred that A. di Cesnola had offered him £3 for the digging-right; he refused it, and as the air of the pit was so foul as to extinguish any light, he filled it in again. Stripped of exaggerations, the story is only that of the opening of a tomb.

well finished: the hair however is rather roughly worked on the crown and back of the head. The end of the nose is the only mutilated feature, and the whole appearance is singularly pleasing.

*Nitoviklia.* Half a mile east of Agia Varvára, on the opposite side of the torrent which runs down from Korovia, a spur of the hills projects into the sea, and its extremity rises into a steep knoll, known as Nitoviklia. Hidden among a mass of undergrowth and 'schinia' both on the knoll and on the ridge immediately below it are ruins which impressed me with a sense of greater antiquity than those of Agia Varvára: they are of much smaller extent, and are confined to a mass of fallen blocks on the knoll and a circular foundation, in places three feet thick and apparently that of a tower, commanding at once the road down the valley on the west and the little bay below. The fallen stones are from three to five feet long by two to three broad and two deep, and very accurately squared and dressed. Further on the ridge below, besides many traces of houses, are two long parallel lines of foundation, resting on solid rock, and now consisting only of a series of blocks, about a foot high, not very closely fitted without mortar. Near them is a deep well, whose walls are lined with unmortared masonry, and in it was found (according to the Korovia villagers) a bronze shovel, now in the possession of Col. Warren, R.A., C.M.G., at Nicosia. This implement belongs certainly to an early period; and it should be remarked that we also picked up on the site three of the flattened crushing-stones, already described at Peristefáni.

With these two groups of ruins I would suggest that the Elisis and Galinóporni tombs are connected. The great distance which intervenes between city and cemetery may be discounted by the following considerations: there is *certainly* no site nearer to the Elisis cave than these, and if the latter was constructed at so great a distance, why not also the Galinóporni graves? It has been found by experience on several Cyprian sites that the older cemeteries often lie at a great distance from the cities, the newer graves filling up the intervening space. Thus the oldest tombs which we opened at Old Paphos lay quite a mile to the east of the city: the graves which honeycomb the bluffs of Ktima undoubtedly belong to New Paphos, distant not much less than a mile: at Arsinoe again the older graves are the most remote. It is well known at what distance from their capitals the tombs of kings are constructed in Egypt and Palestine, and it seems not unreasonable to suppose that the great Cyprian caves are royal burying-places, carved in the lonely cliff above Elisis, and in the strange contorted strata of Galinóporni, at a like distance from the city on the coast. The inaccessible position of the former has caused it to remain solitary, but round the latter scores of lesser graves were cut, the rock being unusually adapted for the purpose by its softness and durability[1]: indeed it is possible that none so good exists nearer to the city.

*Kiouria.*

We may now proceed rapidly up the remainder of the southern coast to Cape Dinaretum, for there are no other remains of much importance on this side of the Carpass. Leaving Galinóporni and striking the path to Rizo-Karpaso the site of an ancient village is seen on the right just before entering the Sykadhes plain. The most noticeable feature is a pair of sarcophagi, one complete (but rifled), the other broken into two pieces: the chests of the sarcophagi and the lids are each cut out of a single piece of the native limestone, the former being neither inscribed nor ornamented in any way. The lids are of the usual pattern. The dimensions of the chests are 7 ft. 4 in. × 3 ft. 5 in. × 3 ft. 8 in., and the lids are 1 ft. 6 in. high. The walls are six inches thick. Both appeared to me to be Roman or Byzantine. Half a mile east again, on a flat-topped hill, known as Mesovouni, are several earth-graves, probably belonging to this village: they were accidentally revealed a short time ago to the owner of the soil while ploughing, one of his oxen treading through into a grave. Glass and inferior jewellery and pottery were found in all that were explored.

*Chelones.*

*Καρπασίαι νῆσοι.*

On the sea-coast, at the mouth of the Karamani stream, are the ruins of a small village of Byzantine period, and at 'Aphendrika[2]' in the plain is a dilapidated church of unusual size, surrounded by traces of a cloister. The next point of interest is Chelones, which should be marked on the Survey Map at Agia Pappou. Here is a considerable rock, known as *Ἄσπρο νησί*, and two or three other wave-washed reefs, which are probably the *Νῆσοι Καρπασίαι*, as they lie at a point exactly opposite Carpasia, and at which the width of the isthmus would naturally be measured. The distance, as the crow flies, is rather over

[1] It is noticeable that on the west side of the Galinóporni gully, where the rock changes to a pebbly conglomerate, there are no graves.

[2] Not the better-known site on the coast, some miles to the north-east of this.

three and three-quarter miles, so that Strabo's thirty stadia is wonderfully exact[1].

Beside some late ruins about the ruined shrine of Agia Pappou, curious remains exist a hundred yards to the west of a slip for launching ships down to the sea. Two walls of coarse rubble project from the earthy cliff, and a concrete floor can be seen in section among the detritus which has filled up the space between the walls: the whole has been eaten away by the waves, probably for some distance: but in the clear water I could plainly see an artificially smoothed slope of rock a few feet below the present margin of the water, down which the ships slid into the sea. It is difficult to divine for what purpose such a slip was constructed here,—unless (as Strabo's choice of this, not the narrowest, part of the peninsula for measurement may imply) the cautious mariners of antiquity on their way to and from Salamis sometimes drew their vessels across the neck of land at this point to avoid the dangers of Cape Dinaretum. I saw no corresponding slip at Carpasia, but in a site so much choked with sand it might very well exist unseen; and high as the land is in the centre here, the slope, more especially on the north, is more gentle than at the narrower parts further east. There are instances in the history of ancient navigation of herculean labour undertaken to avoid doubling a headland, sufficient to make the task here seem light by comparison. I examined the valley which runs up towards Rizo-Karpaso, but, if there ever were a plank road, the earth washed down by the torrent has obliterated all trace of it.

*Palaeo-khorio.*

On a round hill known as Palaeokhorío, standing back from the shore a few hundred yards further east, are very considerable débris of houses, a very large ruined church, surrounded by late graves, and one or two plain shafts of columns: the ruins are unusually abundant, covering the whole hill-top with tumbled heaps, but there is every reason to consider them of late period and unimportant. Like the sites that we have just left at Chelones and Karamáni and many others on these coasts, this place was probably abandoned in comparatively modern days, when the ravages of pirates seem almost to have driven the inhabitants from this part of the island altogether[2].

From this point to Cape St. Andréas stretches the wildest and

[1] xiv. 682.

[2] See Pococke's remarks on the desolation of this end of the Carpass, p. 219.

most beautiful portion of the Carpass: the mountainous ridge has become higher and assumed bolder shapes, and its shaggy spurs run out into the sea. Between them for the next few miles lies a succession of tiny fertile plains, destitute of inhabitants except at harvest-time, and fringing sandy bays, on the very margin of which sweet water can be found at the depth of a few feet, while the wells further inland are brackish. In one such plain an hour eastward from Rizo-Karpaso lies Platia, a little summer-hamlet built upon and out of the ruins of an earlier settlement; on the left a great isolated block of a brilliant red colour stands up among the forest, and somewhere among these hills copper has been found, for on the shore in the bay of Nankomi I picked up slags similar to those at Limni in Papho.

Presently the little plains and bays come to an end, and the shaggy ridge bends round to the sea, falling in perpendicular cliffs right into deep water. There is no longer a road along the gullies and low ground, and we climb on to a rugged plateau which gradually slopes again to the eastern cape: the little monastery of the Apostolos Andréas, the islands called the 'Keys of Cyprus,' and a knob of rock standing upon Cape St. Andréas itself come into view, and far away over a stretch of windless burnished sea the blue cone of Mount Casius in Syria rises out of the haze. A quarter of an hour before reaching the extremity we passed the ruins of a village on the edge of the cliff, now known as Agios Iannis and quite modern, and were soon established in the guest-room of the Monastery, lately entirely rebuilt by the care and munificence of its Oeconomus[1]. Situated at the world's end, on a burning plateau of rock and scrub, it has almost no inhabitants: one solitary monk and two δοῦλοι were alone in it during my visit, seeing no one but a chance traveller, or the sailors who land to get water

*Apostolos Andréas.*

[1] This monastery is said to owe its foundation to St. Andrew, who, landing on the island, found here a spring by which he set up two stones. The additional legend, mentioned by Mrs. Scott-Stevenson (p. 295), that he was conveying the sacred Kykkou picture, I did not hear, and I doubt if it be a genuine legend at all, as the provenance of that picture from Constantinople in the eleventh century is well known in Cyprus. It has however a historical interest, as having been the last refuge of Isaac Comnenus, who probably fled hither in the hope of finding conveyance to Cilicia or Syria. From Roger de Hoveden's account it would appear that Richard himself received Isaac's surrender at this lonely spot. Bishop Stubbs has wrongly accused the chronicler of confounding 'Candare' with 'Caput Sancti Andreae': although the expression 'fortissima' suits the former better. Still the words of Hoveden are explicit, and besides Kantara was not an abbatia.

at the spring under the tiny church of St. Andrew, from which the Monastery derives its sanctity and its fame. From time to time a sponge-boat fishes in the bay, and I made use of one to procure conveyance to the Kleides Islands for the investigation of the reported (but wholly fictitious) antiquities thereupon. I had first tried an Arab caique which had called for water, and indeed concluded a bargain with its captain to take me thither at daybreak: but a fair wind springing up at sunset tempted him, and taking advantage of my departing for a bathe, he sailed away with the narghilé which I had lent to him in token of our contract concluded! A Symiote sponge-fisher proved less perfidious, and next morning I was rowed out to the islands, coasting round the cliffs, and looking down through two hundred feet of clear sea on to every shell or weed upon the bottom. But I had to be contented with the marvellous scenes of the voyage, for the islands afforded me nothing more than a superb view of the Cilician and Syrian coasts divided by a hazy gap which marked the bay of Iskenderun. Three of the six islands are mere reefs washed from end to end by the swell which seems to heave always round Cape St. Andréas: of the remainder, one is very small, not more than a few yards in diameter, but just raised enough out of the water to support a scanty vegetation; another, somewhat larger, is divided from the mainland by a channel only a few feet wide, and is a mere mass of shingle cemented together and covered with stunted undergrowth; the last and largest lies nearly a mile out, and is covered with 'schinia' shrubs and grass, and inhabited by countless sea-birds. On its northern side reeds and rank grass indicate a dried spring, but I searched every inch of the ground without finding a tomb, a hewn stone, a cut rock, or any trace of ancient inhabitation whatsoever.

*Kleides Islands.*

On our way back to the Monastery we boarded the caique whose boat we had been using, and after I had been treated to sailors' twist and villainous rum at midday in July, the trawl was hauled in for my edification. Boats like this, using simply a heavy drag-net, form the lowest grade, paying only £3 10*s.* to the island revenue; whereas if diving apparatus of any sort be used, the impost would be £30. The trawler may get as many as fifty sponges a-day, ranging in value from a piastre up to three shillings; but the damage that is done meanwhile to the fishery is incalculable, if by each haul thirty miniature sponges are torn off the bottom to every three or four matured and worth retaining! Such at least was the case that morning, for among the strange sea things which came up with the net were some thirty sponges in all, of which three only were approved by the fishermen. A paternal administration should look to this: the Fishery properly preserved and farmed might be a very lucrative perquisite of the Cyprian Exchequer.

*Temple of Aphrodite Acraea.*

From the Monastery it is an hour's journey to the extremity of Cape Dinaretum, where rises the mass called the Castros—Pococke's 'rock of marbles of different colours stretching into the sea,' upon which he observed 'signs of foundations of a building.' These foundations I also saw, though they have been much robbed since Pococke's time to supply material for the rebuilding of the Monastery; nothing is now left but traces of an oblong, about 117 ft. × 57 ft., set nearly true east and west, and therefore crosswise as regards the top of the little mount which lies about N.E. and S.W.[1]. Within these foundations one or two attempts have been made to dig, but to no great depth. Down the western slope of the rock (which falls a hundred feet sheer to the sea on the other three sides) various remains of the building above have fallen or been rolled. Among heaps of squared stones I noticed a pedestal of blue limestone, uninscribed; a headless stone statue, female, and with the arms close to the sides, in the stiff archaic position and of the same rude workmanship that I had observed at Peristefáni; and near it a draped leg of a later period.

These then are the remains of the Temple of Aphrodite Acraea, for Strabo's words are clear: *ἡ δ' ἀκρώρεια καλεῖται Ὄλυμπος, ἔχουσα Ἀφροδίτης Ἀκραίας ναὸν, ἄδυτον γυναιξὶ καὶ ἀόρατον, πρόκεινται δὲ πλησίον αἱ Κλεῖδες, κ.τ.λ.*: and this hillock is that dignified by the name of Olympus, the *σεμνὰ κλιτὺς Ὀλύμπου*[2] alluded to by Euripides in the Bacchae (409) as an abode of desire, and is certainly the original of Claudian's imaginative description of the mountain and grove of Venus (Epithal. Hon. et Mar. 49 sqq.):

> 'Mons latus eoum Cypri praeruptus obumbrat
> Invius humano gressu; Phariumque cubile
> Proteos et septem despectat cornua Nili,' etc.

That the Temple was *ἄδυτον γυναιξὶ καὶ ἀόρατον* probably

[1] Sakellarios, vol. i. pp. 150 foll., has a fair description of this.

[2] The only Cyprian mountain which retains the name of Olympus in modern days is one of the peaks of the Northern Range behind Akanthou: but there is no reason to believe that the names of this line of peaks are old; cf. 'Sina,' 'St. Hilarion,' etc.

G 2

means that *married* women were excluded from its rites, while maidens there underwent the initiation which Herodotus records at Babylon, adding, *ἐνιαχῇ δὲ καὶ τῆς Κύπρου ἐστὶ παραπλήσιος τούτῳ νόμος*[1]. We are never likely to learn more of it, for there is no scope for excavation, the site having been too thoroughly plundered either to rebuild the monastery, or, like Famagusta, to make the quays and hotels of Port Said.

At the foot of the rock remains of a town extend for some distance inland: immediately to the south stood a large building, among whose ruins is a plain cap of 1 ft. 6 in. diameter: but the whole site has been much quarried. Several rock-tombs covered by lids, but of a different type and later period than those at Galinóporni, lie near the latter building, and others are in the hill behind. Along the northern shore ancient wheel-marks are distinctly visible, and two subterranean pools, to which access is obtained by flights of steps, lie on the south of this road. There remain to be mentioned only two artificial grots in the northern face of the Temple rock, but I failed to get into either, one being blocked by the falling-in of the rock, the other inaccessible without a ladder. I could see that the roof of each was blackened by smoke, and they may have been the abode of hermits, who seem to entertain a predilection for remote headlands. Engel (vol. i. p. 156) suggests that the town of Acra mentioned by Stephen of Byzantium (s. v.) should be placed here: no other situation has ever been assigned to it (except by Sakellarios), and the epithet *ἄκραια* is slightly in favour of an identification with these ruins, while their position on Cape Dinaretum is such as one would suggest for an '*Ἄκρα*[2].' Still this is slender evidence whereon to base the identification of a town whose bare name is mentioned once only; and it must be remembered that *ἄκραια* is a standing epithet of Aphrodite at Cnidus and Troezen, and of Hera at Argos and elsewhere.

Late in the afternoon of July 18th we began the westward journey down the northern coast, with difficulty threading our way through a luxuriant forest of arbutus, schinia, and flowering thorns, the path now following the windings of the fretted coast-line, and presently striking in to the hills, when they approached too near to the sea to allow farther passage. Nothing of more interest is to be seen on the way than the small site of Palaeokhani, whose oil-stones and well are indicative of an ancient

[1] i. 199.

[2] Cf. Strabo, loc. cit.: *εἶτ' ἄκρα καὶ ὄρος.*

farm, until after four hours' journey we reach Aphendrika[1], a mere cluster of huts, around and among which lie ruins which are probably those of Urania.

Urani

Neither Strabo nor Ptolemy makes mention of this city, nor do they note anything at all between Carpasia and Cape Dinaretum: and, but for a doubtful reference in Nonnus (xiii. 450), our only authority for its existence is Diodorus (xx. 47), who relates its capture κατὰ κράτος by Demetrius Poliorcetes. His previous phrase—τοῖς πλησιοχώροις προσβολὰς ποιησάμενος—suggests that it lay at no great distance from Carpasia where Demetrius landed, while we are led to suppose that it was the place of next importance, fortified or possessing an acropolis. To my knowledge there are two sites only at this end of the Carpass whose remains are sufficient for such a town, that at Agia Varvára, already described, and this at Aphendrika: the latter is distinctly the more important of the two, and possesses a stronger citadel, while it is also much nearer to Carpasia (four miles distant as against eleven), and would more naturally be connected with it. The words of Diodorus by no means imply that Demetrius took these cities *on his way to* Salamis; rather he seems to have made a preliminary raid and returned to his ships. For these reasons accordingly, failing all assistance from the geographers, I would identify Urania with the ruins at Aphendrika.

There is a narrow strip of fertile plain between the hills and the sea, and the ruins lie back from the coast on the last slopes of the ridge, covering a considerable area with masses of squared stone, fragments of columns, and foundations of houses. Three large Byzantine churches are prominent objects, the principal one, dedicated to the Panagia Chrysiotissa, having a threefold apse, and being much larger than modern village churches. In the precinct of a second, that of Agios Demetrios, lie fragments of granite columns of Roman period and a marble cippus uninscribed; and the sites of three other churches can be traced, proving that Urania (if so it be) was a place of considerable importance in the Byzantine period. East of the town may be seen the large quarry from which it was built, now called the 'Phylakes,' and behind the ruins rises the citadel, of no great height but a very conspicuous object, projecting sheer on three sides from the hills into the plain.

[1] Pococke's 'Asphronisy.' I failed to see his 'wall running down to the sea': what remains there were of it are probably built into cottages by this time.

The summit of this rock bears ancient remains as interesting and perhaps as primitive as anything in Cyprus, for the entire ground-plan of the building, whether palace or fortress, which once crowned it, has been preserved by the fact that the lower portion of all its chambers were excavated in the living rock, to a depth of from 2 to 4 ft. The walls are therefore so far intact as to determine the position of the doorways and the character of the approaches: the outer walls are generally 2 to 2½ ft. thick, and the party-walls vary from 1 to 1½ ft., but no trace is left of the masonry, which must have been superimposed. From the appended plan it will be seen that the building was approached from the south-east by a gate and wide passage, on the left of which are two chambers: a flight of four steps and another gate whose sockets remain lead into an inner chamber, which again opens into a third, the largest of all. On the east a considerable 'margin' of uncut rock has been left, and a smaller one on the right, but on the north, overlooking the city, the precipice falls away sheer from the outer wall of the chamber.

To this rock-cut dwelling it is difficult not to assign great antiquity: this eminence must always have been the acropolis of any city built here (for nature has provided no other), and on such acropolis must have been a fortress. Now the fact that a tomb belonging to this site bears a Cypriote inscription of a particularly archaic character[1] proves the existence of the town at an early period, and these rock-chambers must be coeval with its foundation. They recalled to me the strange remains of a similar fortress, cut to a depth of several feet in the living rock of the acropolis of Kumbet in Phrygia, and ascribed by Professor W. M. Ramsay to the same period as the neighbouring city of Midas[2]: and I have little doubt that the plan of a fortress or dwelling-place constructed by very early Asiatic immigrants into Cyprus has been preserved at Aphendrika.

At a distance of barely half-a-mile below the city lies a little horseshoe bay which served as harbour: the entrance is only a few yards in width, and the space within would afford room for many vessels of small draught. On the beach still stand four mooring-posts of stone, three feet high and two in diameter,

[1] Published by MM. Beaudouin and Pottier in the Bulletin, vol. iii. p. 351, No. 1. To their copy I have nothing to add.

[2] Compare also Professor Ramsay's account of chambers in the citadel of the Lion-City in Phrygia, in Journal of Hell. Studies, vol. ix. p. 353.

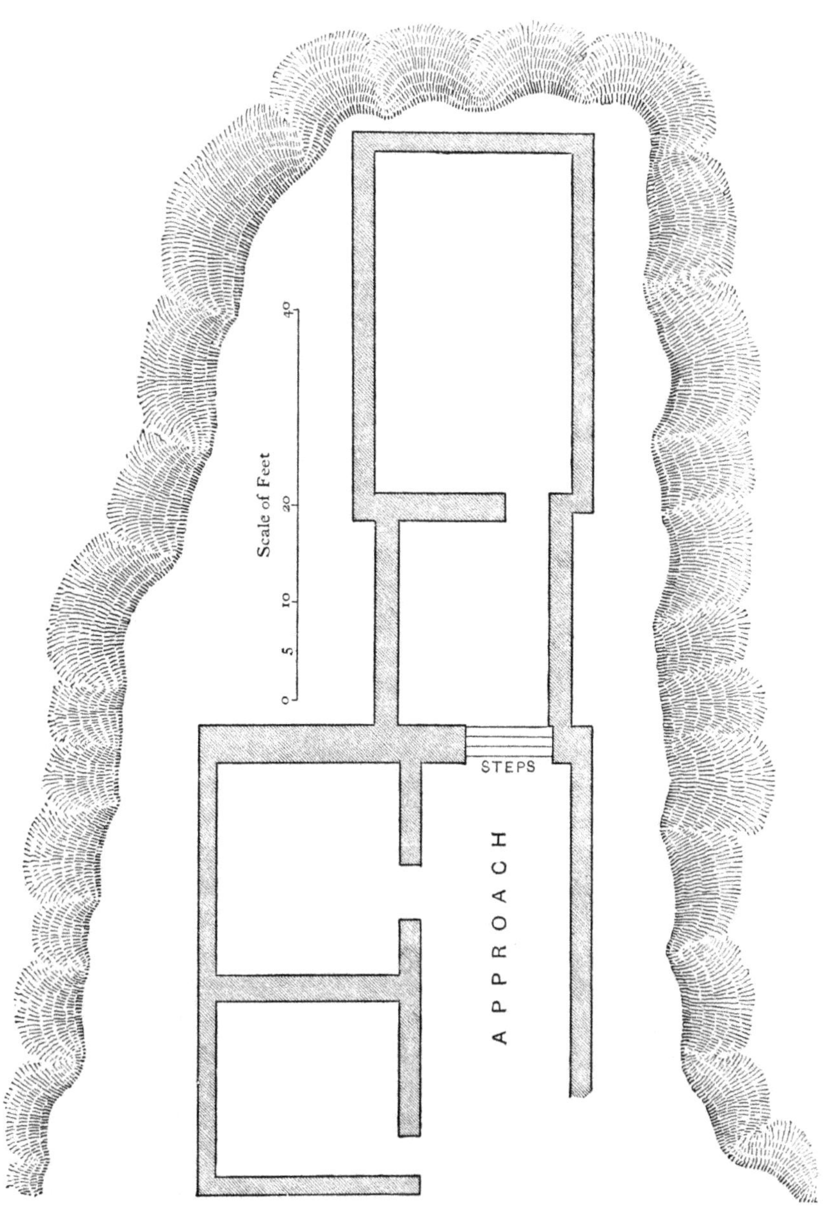


PLAN OF THE FORTRESS AT APHENDRIKA.

and among the heavy sand may be traced for some distance the masonry of the quay. It stands now some yards back from the edge of the water, which has receded, owing either to encroaching sand or to an upheaval of the coast. There are no traces of fortifications about the harbour.

In the western spit of rock and far up into the plain are cut the tombs: many have been opened from time to time by villagers (my own foreman owned to having conducted a little excavation here on his own account before the Occupation), but a vastly greater number are still unexplored, and might throw light on a very early period. The tomb on which the three archaic Cypriote characters (Beaud. and Pott., loc. cit., Sammlung, No. 143) are cut has a curious expanding δρόμος: the other inscriptions published by MM. Beaudouin and Pottier I did not see, the sand having probably choked up the tombs. A piece of very ornate cornice lies among the bushes, and near it a stone lion, recumbent, and of more than life size: his fore paws are broken off and lie not far away. No tradition of his discovery existed in Aphendrika, and from the evident effects of weather and driving sand I inferred that he had lain above ground for many years. If, as seems most probable, he was taken from a tomb, he may have guarded the sepulchre of a chieftain who held sway over this fertile coast from the acropolis of Urania.

*Agridia.* On the summit of the ridge behind the city has stood a large village of later times, among whose ruins stand the shells of four churches of no special interest. To this securer position the inhabitants of Urania, like those of Carpasia, may have retired to avoid the Arab corsairs. The site is known now as Agridia, and was a fief of the de Verney family.

Another village of earlier date (to judge from a fragment of a stone statue of indifferent workmanship found among the ruins) lay on the coast two miles to the west of Aphendrika; and, riding two miles still in the same direction, we come to the first traces of Carpasia[1].

*Carpasia.* Hellanicus (ap. Steph. Byz. s.v.) and Pliny both rank Carpasia among Phoenician foundations in Cyprus, and certain remains on the plain to the east of the city bear a superficial resemblance to the stone-enclosure of Cnidus. In this case we find three

[1] For ancient references to this city, see Engel, vol. i. pp. 83 foll., and Sakellarios, vol. i. pp. 146 foll.: the latter gives a description of its remains, and so also does Pococke, pp. 218, 219.

enclosures arranged in a group thus, the one leading out of the other:—

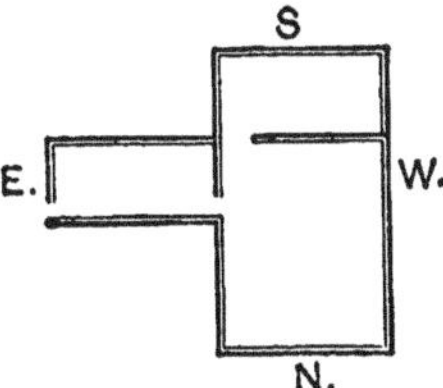


The walls of each are composed of large blocks 3 ft. high, 1 ft. 9 in. thick, and of various lengths from 5 ft. downwards: they are set on edge, and are in no case perfectly contiguous, three or four inches interval being left between each block and its neighbour. That this is due to design and not to displacement is clear from the perfectly perpendicular position of all the stones. To the south are more traces of foundations.

I should hesitate however to assign to this enclosure any mysterious character. Not far from the Monastery of the Apostolos Andréas[1] I had already seen an enclosure, similarly megalithic, but from the presence near it of three unmistakeable 'oil-stones' had concluded at once that it was connected in some way with a press; perhaps had been a store. It should be admitted however that it measured only 12 ft. × 6 ft., and that the stones, though unmortared, were closely fitted, and might well have carried higher courses. Again, in the centre of the site of Carpasia large blocks are to be seen set on end, and not contiguous, round the site of a large church; while in Rizo-Karpaso at this day fences are constructed in precisely this manner. And therefore, while admitting the possibility of this triple enclosure being a sacred *τέμενος*, I feel more disposed to regard it as a cattle-pen, perhaps modern enough.

Such a domestic character should probably be ascribed to an almost square building (30 ft. × 40 ft.) about 200 yards to the south-west. The rock has been hollowed out to a depth of two feet (or probably more, for much rubbish has accumulated in the bottom), and round the edge has been built a wall of large and small blocks to a height of five feet. A number of holes in the inner face of the stones appear to have supported the beams of a light roof. The stones are unmortared and not closely fitted, but otherwise the character of the ruin recalls

[1] At a spot called 'Αλώνια τῆς ἀκαρδινᾶς (?).

that of the Loutron at Salamis, and I would suggest that it has been an ἀποθήκη or fenced cistern.

I need not describe in detail a site on which Sakellarios and Pococke have said so much. For nearly a square mile the slopes below Rizo-Karpaso are strewn with remains, in one place a beautiful monolithic shaft of white marble indicating a building of importance: but all is choked with drifted sand, or earth brought down from above, and the excavator only will be able to make much of the site.

The most remarkable of its features are the Harbour, and the Tombs in the cliffs[1] of Tsambres. The first has been described by the above-mentioned travellers, and I will only add that its pair of artificial moles are the most considerable works of the kind in Cyprus. That on the eastern side can be followed for 370 feet from its starting-place on the shore: it is made for the most part of large squared blocks, formerly riveted to each other by clamps of metal, the marks of which only remain, thus :—

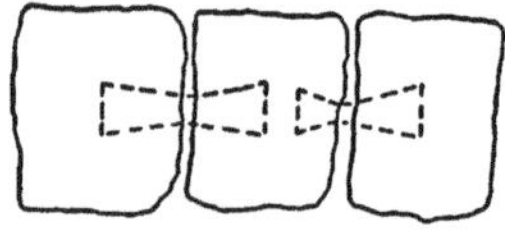

but near the outer end it has been patched in later times with fragments of columns, marble and basalt, clamped together and to the neighbouring blocks, while other drums may be seen through the clear water lower down. The uniform width of the mole is eight feet, and its height above the present water-level about four. It projects from the shore in a north-westerly direction towards the point of the other mole which runs due north; the latter cannot be followed far, but its massive abutment on the shore is probably a fair sample of its character. These works probably attracted Demetrius Poliorcetes, and have caused Strabo to single out for notice the *harbour* of Carpasia.

The eastern headland is strewn with the ruins of the port town, here free from the sand which has buried everything to the west of the ruined church of Agios Philonos, which perhaps represents the cathedral of the bishops of Carpasia in the early days of the see: the present building is however of later date, and appears to have formed part of a monastery. I found in it, besides Roman drums and capitals, a much mutilated female head of no particular interest.

[1] Whence the epithet αἰπεινή applied to Carpasia.

As at Salamis and New Paphos, everything upon the surface of this site is late: but clear evidence of earlier periods in the history of Carpasia is found in the Tombs. Beginning almost as soon as the Harbour is left on the west, they extend for a quarter of a mile right up to the cliffs, which start from the central ridge, and completely shut in the plain on this side. On getting clear of the sand, the ground is seen to be honey-combed with opened graves, from one of which has been excised the following fragment inscribed with Cypriote characters, and now serving for a manger in a stable near the church of St. Synesius at Rizo-Karpaso. The characters are four inches in length and very deeply cut: the excised fragment, which is incomplete on the left, measures 4 ft. 1 in. × 1 ft. 4 in., and has formed the lintel of a rock-cut doorway:

20.

to · | mi · e · | ro · pe · ku · si · na · o

read from the right = 'Ονασικύπρω ἠμι τω . . . .

This, so far as I can discover, is unpublished. Another inscription was reported to have been excised from a tomb at the same time (perhaps the remaining half of the above), but I could not learn what had become of it. Some late intaglios were shown to me in the same village, but as to the provenance of things so portable it is never safe to take the villagers' word.

In the cliff of Tsambres itself are cut a series of fine tombs, certain of which present a feature entirely new to me, and

possibly unique. The face of the rock is carefully scarped, and on the right or left of the tomb doors are left in relief stelae, sometimes singly, sometimes two or three together, sometimes of the conventional shape with pediment, sometimes *anthropoid*, 3 ft. high and 1 ft. 3 in. in breadth at the widest end; but, strange to say, these tablets have never been inscribed. The rock is very hard, its surface intact, the edges of the stelae quite sharp, and mistake is not possible. Were there no more than one example we might conjecture that either the original design was not followed out, or the tomb ultimately received an occupant other than him for whom it was originally hewn: but, having not one but many of these stelae, and finding them in groups on a few tombs only, we must conclude that they are in some way tokens of the dignity or character of the dead; and being carved near the finest tombs, which are hewn out of that part of the necropolis—viz. the cliff itself—which would naturally have been most in request, it is not unreasonable to suppose that they mark the sepulchres of families of very high or even royal rank.

The tombs are all empty, and many, to judge from the crosses cut on walls and roof, have been re-used in Christian times: one is lined with plaster—a precaution whose rarity the tomb-robber may regret—and the doors of others are unusually wide, commensurate in fact with the breadth of the tomb.

There must be a very large number of unopened graves in the plain below Tsambres, and a few weeks might be spent profitably in exploring both them and the city, where the sand is deepest. No scientific work has been done here, and only the early *τυμβωρύχοι*, the villagers, and perhaps Alexander di Cesnola, have ever tried the site.

Another unpublished inscription of Carpasia exists in the ruined church ot Agios Giorgios at Rizo-Karpaso: it is on a pedestal of blue limestone, most difficult to read both from the effects of weather and from being placed in the darkest corner of the building. The lettering is of about the second century B.C., and $\frac{7}{8}$ of an inch in height. The pedestal measures 30 in. x 8 x 30: the last line is broken away.

21. ΛΕΟΝΝΑ // ΟΝ ΤΟΙ //// ΧΙΟΝ ////
ΗΓΕΜΟΝΑΕΠΑΝΔ // ΟΝ //////ΟΙΣΠΑΣΙ
/////////

*Λεόννα[τ]ον τὸν ['Αρ]χίου[ος*
*ἡγεμόνα ἔπανδ[ρ]ον [καὶ τ]οῖς πᾶσι*
*[ἔργοις σπουδαιότατον* . . . . . (vel simile quid).

Probably dedicated by some guild, similar to those at Paphos (the ἀρχιτέκτονες, the περὶ Διόνυσον τεχνῖται, and the like; see Inscriptions of Paphos in the Journal of Hellenic Studies, vol. ix. passim), to its President (ἡγεμών).

*Small sites.* From this point, until we pass out of the Carpass proper into the district of Aphrodisium through the defile above Eptakomi, there is little of archaeological interest. At Selinias, where a tiny spring was still trickling at the end of July, Alexander di Cesnola is said to have found 'a wall and statues': but the plough had obliterated all traces of them[1]. At Vlakhou is a tiny coasting-site, probably mediaeval, such as stud both coasts of the Carpass: and at Pyrgos, twenty minutes' ride into the hills from the summer-hamlet of Makhaeriona, stand the remains of a square tower, probably built as a look-out place for and a refuge from pirates. *Tower at Pyrgos.* Three walls rise to a height of 25 ft.; the fourth has fallen, and the others will soon follow. It is of very poor material and workmanship, and plastered on the inner sides. Near it are two ruined churches and traces of a large village.

*Makhaeriona.* Makhaeriona has a horseshoe bay, shallow and full of reefs; Pococke was told that 'some king antiently resided' there, but no remains are to be seen, and, though I camped there for the night, I learned nothing more of such a tradition.

*Mediaeval sites.* Upon the headland of Akámas, below Gialousa, I saw no remains which would support the theory that here was Teucer's landing-place, Ἀχαιῶν Ἀκτή. Insignificant remains of a village exist on the eastern side of the cape, and traces of a small tower on the western; but both of these, as well as the ruins known as Agios Iannis, close to Gialousa itself, and two sites on a desolate part of the coast below Platanisso, some miles farther to the west, appear to me to be relics of the many stations which maintained commerce with Anatolia in the Middle Ages: ruins of late churches, and small drums of modern columns, may be seen in all the last three that I have mentioned.

As the first peaks of the Northern Range are approached, the country becomes more and more broken, and the coast-road impracticable: the few villages which exist on this side, Agios

[1] It was here that Pococke saw 'remains of columns four feet in diameter': if he was not mistaken in the character of what he saw, and if he really means 'diameter,' they are very much larger than any others in the island. The villagers also have a tradition about the place.

Andronikos, Kilanemos, Platanisso and Eptakomi, nestle behind the ridge in deep valleys, or on sheltered plateaux, raising crops of cotton, gourds, melons and all kinds of vegetables, wherever there is water at hand.

Across the base of the Carpass the mountains stretch like a wall, terminating in the huge buttress of Mount Yioudhi, which bars all ingress to the narrow strip—the garden of Cyprus—which extends for fifty miles between mountains and sea, past Aphrodisium, Macaria, Kerynia and Lapethus to Cape Crommyon and the bay of Soli. Above Eptakomi, pleasantest and most hospitable of Carpass villages, a narrow defile leads into this favoured land, well judged by Colonel Leake to be the most beautiful part of the Turkish Empire, and somewhere towards its eastern extremity the site of Aphrodisium is to be sought.

*Aphrodisium.* This point being of some importance and hitherto quite undecided, it may be considered somewhat minutely. Ancient authorities are seldom adequate for the exact determination of questions in geography, and this case is no exception. Strabo mentions it next after Lapethus: εἶτ' Ἀφροδίσιον καθ' ὃ στενὴ ἡ νῆσος· εἰς γὰρ Σαλαμῖνα ὑπέρβασις σταδίων ἑβδομήκοντα· εἶτ' Ἀχαιῶν ἀκτή, κ.τ.λ. But the distance of *any* point on this coast from Salamis is not less than sixteen miles, or double Strabo's estimate. Ptolemy places it between Ἀχαιῶν ἀκτή and Macaria, but as the site of the former is equally unknown, and of the latter not too well assured, this does not help us much. Stephen of Byzantium calls it Aphrodisias, and mentions it tenth among cities of that name, but adds no details. It was not the Throne of a Bishop, and therefore Hierocles and the Notitiae do not help us.

Strabo then is the only authority who attempts precise indication, and he tells us no more than that it lay at the base of the Carpass and at or about the point of the northern coast nearest to Salamis.

Remains still exist of three sites and three sites only in this district which can be said to fulfil these conditions in any way: that at Galounia, two miles east of Davlos; that known as Pergamon or Ypsiló, nearly due north of Akanthou; and a third two miles farther east, and known as Iastriká. All three are about equidistant from Salamis, and may be roughly said to lie at that very ill-defined locality, the base of the Carpass.

We must attempt to judge then by the internal evidence of the sites themselves, by the character and importance of the ruins, by any indications to be drawn from individual objects found upon any one of them, and by the quality of their harbours: for it may be at once premised that the most satisfactory kind of evidence, a survival of the ancient name either in a modern title or an inscription, is not available in this case.

The easternmost site, Galounia, has been generally accepted as that of Aphrodisium [1], probably because it lies more exactly at the base of the Carpass than the others. The actual ruins are insignificant and cover a very small area, not more than 200 yds. x 100. The schinia shrubs make search very difficult on all these deserted sites, but I succeeded in exploring the tumbled heaps of stone (much of it unsquared) without finding anything more sumptuous than a fragment of a stone triglyph, three plain broken columns of small diameter, and plenty of glazed and unglazed red potsherds. A very small aqueduct may still be traced from the ruins of a plastered ἀποθήκη up to a spring among the foot-hills, now known as Thepos, to the east of which is a little village site, conspicuous for nothing but 'oil-stones.' The harbour lies on the eastern side of the ruins, and is formed by an elbow of the land, and a long reef running eastward, its shape therefore being an oblong open only to the east. The reef is now two or three feet below the mean sea-level, but being formed of soft argillaceous rock, it may have suffered from the continual assaults of the waves. On the outside it is further protected by the Galounia islands. This natural basin is still fairly deep, and has continued to be a landing-place, if I may judge from the host of modern Greek initials cut in the soft rock about it. There is however no trace of any human handiwork, either in the shape of quays, warehouses, mooring-posts, or the like, and it must be confessed that the harbour would be most difficult to enter during westerly winds (the prevailing direction in Cyprus), and anything but sheltered from either the north or east. I saw no tombs, and they may be yet to be found.

*Galounia.*

It is just possible that Strabo either stated, or intended to state, the distance from Aphrodisium to the *bay* of Salamis, and not to Salamis itself: if so, Galounia has strong claims, for

[1] E.g. both by Sakellarios (vol. i. p. 143) and General di Cesnola (Cyprus, p. 239): of the latter's 'plateau presenting the remains of an extensive town with Corinthian capitals and fluted columns in marble and blue granite lying half buried in the soil,' I saw and heard nothing; nor is there any 'pier.'

it is distant as the crow flies from the southern coast of the Carpass just Strabo's 79 stadia, or 8½ miles; whereas both the other sites are four or five miles farther removed from the nearest point of the Bay. But as this involves an emendation of Strabo's text, it must not be pressed; and on other grounds I cannot feel satisfied that the alteration is worth the making. The ruins at Galounia are insignificant in the extreme: one would have looked for remains of marble, or of large buildings; but here not only are there none, but it is very improbable from the nature of the ground that there is anything still buried, the rock being everywhere near the surface. The site and its aqueduct are alike those of a village or a small 'scala,' and the harbour is ill-formed even by nature, and has not been bettered by man. I arrived at Galounia fully prepared to accept it as Aphrodisium, but left it with the conviction that, while it might be Ἀχαιῶν Ἀκτή, the larger city was to be found further west. Its vicinity to the pass of Eptakomi, the shortest and easiest route to Salamis from the north coast, makes it very natural that it should have been selected by the logographers as the landing-place of Teucer.

*Pergamon.* The central site of the three, Pergamon or Ypsilo (so called from the knoll which rises to the north), lies about nine miles to the west, and within an hour's ride of Akanthou. It has been described by Sakellarios (vol. i. p. 141), who imagined it to be the site of Urania—a very unlikely suggestion;—but Pococke seems to have missed all these sites through following the higher road close under the mountains. A new traveller however takes his place, namely Ross[1], who enumerates its main characteristics, and identifies it with Aphrodisium. General di Cesnola mentions it without comment. Two points tell for Ross's theory, as against Sakellarios'—the greater extent of the ruins as compared with Galounia, and the presence of a sort of acropolis, on which are some evidences of man's handiwork not unlike those at Aphendrika, but much smaller. I should imagine that the hillock had originally been quarried to build the city. There are distinct traces of the top of the hill having been cut completely away, a single pillar of rock—7½ ft. high, by 4 at the base and 3 at the top—having been left near the centre of the summit. Near it two oblong depressions, one higher than the other, have been cut into the

[1] Reise auf Kos und Cypern, p. 135.

gentle slope of the rock, and they communicate by steps with each other and with the higher part of the rock beyond. The relation of each to the other is shown in the woodcut.

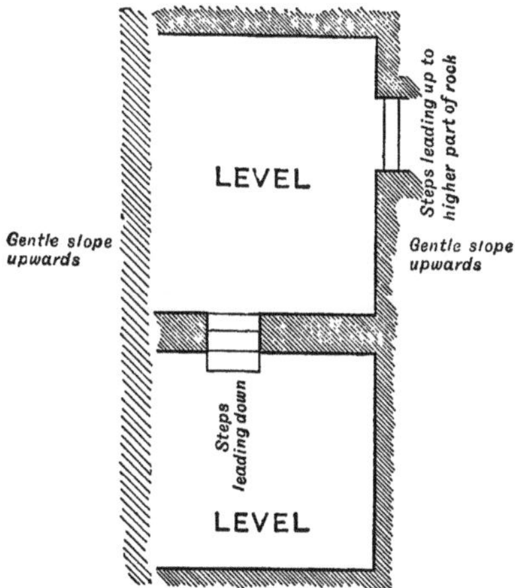


At their deepest end they are not more than two feet below the general level of the rock, and what purpose they or the rock-pillar have served is not very clear. The latter may be a menhir, but I doubt it, and the best suggestion that I can offer as to the former is that they are ancient threshing-floors. It should be added that a huge oil-stone lies not far away, and that the other remains upon the site are not such as to suggest extreme antiquity.

After a careful exploration of the heaps of ruins which represent the ancient town, and which extend south of the knoll as far as the little church of Panagia Pergaminiotissa, I can state that the following exist on the site :—

The ruins of at least one church.

Only small columns of rough stone, and plain late capitals.

Plain unglazed red pottery only.

Stones bearing late masons' marks, e.g. Y and A.

Four pierced monoliths, two built into a fence, the other two in situ, standing side by side, 3 ft. 8 in. apart. They deserve particular notice because they *face* one another, thus bringing the two slits opposite in such a manner that a beam might have been passed through them, as in a modern oil-press. Near them is a rock-cut tank.

A tiny subterranean church cut in the rock. It is divided by a rock-cut iconostasis; and measures only 16½ ft. x 13ft.

Many tombs, some roofed with slabs quite after the modern manner; a plain sarcophagus stands on the side of a mound, having probably been taken from a tomb but abandoned by the riflers as not worth the trouble of carriage.

Ross had been told in Nikosia of an inscription, which he failed to find here, probably because it never existed. A Cypriote if asked for *πέτραι γραμμέναι* will report them any where, for chance scratches, mouldings, flutings, as well as letters, rank with him under the common class, *γράμματα.* I was assured at Akanthou that nothing had ever been found here, and the peasants have a tradition that the old church of Panagia Pergaminiotissa is coeval with the surrounding ruins. For my own part I believe that this is not far from the truth, and that Pergamon—however it came by its name—is a Byzantine site, and most certainly not Aphrodisium. No harbour exists at any near point of the coast, although there are slight remains of a village at Agios Perperos on the cliff top a quarter of a mile below Pergamon: my guide averred that fragments of statuary and terra-cottas had been unearthed here, but discovering that he was the owner of this particular piece of land, I was less inclined to believe him than I should have been even under ordinary circumstances.

*Iastriká.* The third possible site is situated about three miles further west, at the mouth of the stream which runs down from Akanthou. Its modern name, as I understood it, is *Iastriká* or *Giastriká*, but Sakellarios calls it *Λιαστρικά*[1], and Cesnola *Gastria.* The ruins, which have been quarried to build the large village of Akanthou, cover a headland which here separates two bays. The end of the cape has been almost entirely stripped, but farther inland the heaps of stone are thicker, and there is obviously a great deal still buried. The Akanthiotes aver that since the memory of man they have plundered the place, and have always found large squared stones and marble; and that a pedestal with an inscription was found many years ago, but impounded by the Archbishop and removed to Nikosia[2]. Among the ruins I found a half-buried stone cippus, and turning it

[1] Sakellarios, educated Greek as he was, strangely distorts names: witness Ἔψηλο for the obvious Ὕψηλο, Γροτῆρι for Ἀκροτῆρι, etc.

[2] This *may* be Ross's Pergamon inscription; vid. *supra.*

over read the following inscription in lettering 1½ inches in length:—

| 22. | ΑΡΙΣΤϹΛΛΟΣ | Ἀριστ(ό)λ(α)ος |
|---|---|---|
| | ΠΑΥΣΑΝΙΟΥ | Παυσανίου |
| | ΘΕΣΣΑΛΟΣ | Θεσσαλός. |

On the western side of the headland is a perfectly-shaped horseshoe bay, all but landlocked by high cliffs—the best natural harbour in this part of Cyprus, and sheltered from every wind. I saw however no trace of quays.

Without excavation no more is to be seen, and it is rash to speak decidedly. But to my mind the evidence of the harbour, of the inscription, of tradition, and of the size and possibilities of the site all tend to its identification with Aphrodisium: from Salamis it is about equidistant with Galounia, and the island might easily be said to become στενή from this point. It is also worth notice that whereas no modern settlement has succeeded to Galounia, the chief place of all this district has grown out of Iastriká. Akanthou stands in the same relation to it as Rizo-Karpaso to Carpasia, Agridia to Urania, modern Lapithos to the ancient, and Ktima to New Paphos.

*Kako-scale.*

We must dismiss very briefly two small sites in the neighbourhood of Iastriká;—one, a spot on the left bank of the Akanthou stream, ten minutes below the village and known as Kako-scale, where fragments of polychromatic statuettes are frequently turned up by the plough. Gregorio and myself picked up half-a-dozen such, on which the bands of colour were very distinct. The same class of remains may be found on many Cyprian sites, e.g. at the mouth of the Limniti river and near Kalorgá (vid. *infra*), and probably indicates the position of a small shrine, in this case about a mile and a-half from the walls of Aphrodisium. The other site is called Elaopotámi, and lies midway between Akanthou and Pergamon, among the charub-trees which cover all this low ground. A fragment of a marble column, the ruins of a church, and some large squared blocks are its main features: it is of very small extent, and can have been no more than a hamlet.

*Elaopotámi.*

*Tomb near Phlamoudhi.*

But we must return to the neighbourhood of Davlos to describe a remarkable tomb, excavated out of the level rock, and, so far as I could discover, absolutely solitary. It is situated in the middle of the forest, about half an hour due north of Phlamoudhi, and a couple of hundred yards only from the sea. Some small remains of an ancient village are to be seen something less than a mile away to the east, but their character is far too mean for this sumptuous tomb, and I am fain to connect it with Aphrodisium, distant as it is, and to suppose it to be a royal sepulchre. The accident of losing my way in the forest brought me to the place, no villager at Davlos having appeared to be aware of its existence, and since no traveller but myself has seen it, it is worth a detailed description.

The tomb has a square court—12 ft. 6 in. each way—sunk to a depth of 6 ft. 6 in. into the rock, and open to the sky. On the western and northern sides of this run covered colonnades, 5 ft. 6½ in. in breadth, each supported by two fluted Doric columns, and a double column at the common corner, all cut

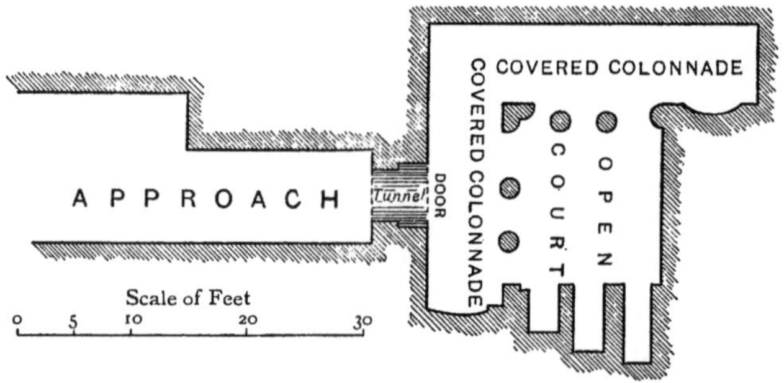


out of the solid rock. The colonnade on the north is continued eastwards for 5 ft. 7 in. into the rock, and perhaps the recess so formed contained a body. Similarly the western colonnade is continued southwards. The columns have supported a small architrave and frieze, with triglyphs and plain metopes; but all are much mutilated. The eastern side of the court is a blank wall, but on the southern, three sepulchral niches, the longest measuring 5 ft. 6 in. × 3 ft. 2 in. × 3 ft. 6 in., penetrate into the rock. Crosses have been cut everywhere by pious Christian hands to conjure the evil spirits of the old sepulchre.

Entrance is gained by a *δρόμος*, nearly 30 ft. long, which slopes gradually downwards and tunnels under the western wall, thus opening into the west colonnade. The plan above will make these details more clear, and it will be seen that the whole tomb could contain five bodies at least. The *δρόμος* is much choked with earth, but there is not much accumulation in the tomb itself. I took photographs from above and inside the tomb itself, but, in common with all taken in July, they have failed.

Similar tombs exist in Cyprus only in the Palaeocastro near New Paphos, one of which is described by General di Cesnola (p. 224). The two examples there are each larger than this near Phlamoudhi, but do not excel it in carefulness of construction; indeed, as Pococke would say, the latter is 'a very particular piece of work,' remarkable for its exact proportions and its remote and lonely situation. It is difficult to assign to it an exact date, but the use of the pure Doric order is very rare, if not unknown (to judge from existing remains) in Cyprus after Ptolemaic times.

*Kantara Castle.*

The superb castle of Kantara, the Hundred Chambers, which, seeming to hang in mid-air, dominates this end of Cyprus, has been often visited and described. Buffavento stands higher, and St. Hilarion can show more perfect ramparts and turrets, but neither recalls so strangely a forgotten age, neither seems to be so thickly peopled with its ghosts, as this lonely ruin on its pillar of rock. No painter's wildest fancy has pictured anything so fantastic as these Cyprian castles, and, standing at the foot of the last steep leading to the gate of Kantara, and involuntarily recalling the fairy-towers of romance, the traveller might imagine it the stronghold of a Sleeping Beauty, untouched by change or time for a thousand years! It is best seen from the north-west, where the precipice is sheerest, the winding walls seem to cling most dizzily to its face, and the ruins of the interior cannot be seen; but once within the outer gate the illusion partly vanishes in view of the broken battlements, although man and horse can still find shelter in many of the chambers.

On the peak of the rock has stood a little windy chapel, now destroyed by frost and rain, wherefrom may be seen the finest view in Cyprus. To the east the jagged outline of the Carpass, dividing two seas; to the south the bay of Salamis, in whose recess a yellow patch shows the situation of Famagusta; and westwards the vast brown level of the Mesaoréa, with just a glimmer of the southern sea and the peaks of Stavrovouni and Machaeras closing the view. On either hand the saw-like ridge of the Northern Range, on the one side declining in shaggy steps to the broken ground of the Carpass, on the other bending in a blue semicircle to Cape Cormachiti. On the north a stretch of indented coast-line and blue sea, and beyond the enormous mass of the Karamanian Taurus, piled up ridge upon ridge, dark lines marking the gullies, and white patches the desolate uplands far into the interior of Anatolia. It is a matchless view, not because it is more extensive than Buffavento or Troodos afford—nay, rather its radius is less—but because of the wilder outlines of the coast, the double sea, the silence and desolation of the prospect. Under Buffavento lie Kyrenia and Nicosia; Troodos is too far above the prospect, and its sloping sides do not appal like the abysmal precipices of Kantara, whence hardly a glimpse of human habitation dispels the illusion of an enchanted castle, asleep in a sleeping land.

Its early history has not been written: no one knows precisely who built it and when: perhaps it was the Byzantine governors during the era of Arab inroads. The presence of a spring of fresh water below the summit must always have given it an advantage over the other two castles, but it opened its gates without awaiting attack after St. Hilarion had capitulated to Richard. During the next four centuries it was taken and retaken by the partisans of Frederick II, by Philip of Navarre, and by the Genoese, until the Venetians finally reduced it to its present condition of ruin.

The plain of Davlos, Phlamoudhi, and Akanthou is the richest charub and grain district in the island. A special assessment is assigned by the Revenue officers to its crop, and, after tithe has been taken, each peasant stores his surplus in funnel-shaped pits, called 'vouphes,' dug in the clay or soft rock, and baked by a fire lighted inside—similar to those found on the site of the temple at Paphos. But much prosperity has hardened the hearts of the natives, and I met nowhere with such scant civility and such stolid reticence as in Akanthou. The untutored rascality of the Paphiti and the simple ignorance of the Carpasiotes are both to be preferred to the more civilised cunning of the Greeks of the centre of Cyprus.

*Macaria.* We have already passed the proper limits of the Carpass, but it will be well to continue for a few miles to the west, to reach the site of Macaria. The headland of Moulos on which lie its ruins projects abruptly into the sea and forms a fine situation for a city: the harbour (if it is worthy the name) lay on the eastern side, and remains exist of buildings near the water's edge, and perhaps of a quay: but the bay is very shallow, full of reefs, and unsheltered, and can never have been much frequented. The remains of the city are among the least interesting in Cyprus; a mere wilderness of rubble, small stone shafts, red and buff potsherds, oil-stones, and pierced monoliths. The number of the latter is extraordinary; I counted no less than six on the site, all less than six feet high. The oil-stones usually lay near them. I was disappointed with the character of the ruins, for this site had been reported a good field for excavation, while the identity of its name, Macaria, with one of the synonyms of the whole island, and its possible connection with Makar or Melkarth had encouraged hopes of finding important and early antiquities: early it may be, important it certainly was not, as indeed its omission by Strabo and all ancient authorities, except Ptolemy, proves: and it is needless to point out that any theory that all Cyprus was called Macaria either by or because of the inhabitants of this little coast-town, is probably an inversion of the truth. Still there is a remarkable point of correspondence with Phoenicia in the fashion of certain tombs south-west of the city (and already alluded to p. 76 in connection with the cemetery of Galinóporni), which are sunk into the rock and covered with ordinary sarcophagus lids, not resting on sills, but on the top of the rock. To these graves, of which there are only half-a-dozen, I know no parallel in Cyprus; but M. Rénan[1] describes their counterpart at Maschnaka, near Byblos.

A short distance from this cluster we found among the undergrowth a fragment of a sepulchral stone stele, bearing a draped female figure, nearly life-size, and in very high relief. The right foot is crossed over the left, and the left elbow has rested on some support, perhaps an urn. The head is wanting, the hands are mutilated, and the whole is much weathered; but enough remains to show that the relief was of a better period and of finer workmanship than most Cyprian statuary. The treatment of the drapery shows a great advance on the Peristefáni draped figures, while it is as much superior to the Roman statuary found near Kythrea, and now in the Government Offices at Nicosia. The length of the fragment, as it lies, is 4 ft. 3 in., but a piece has been broken off from both ends. It may have stood upright after the manner of the Ceramicus reliefs, or, were it about 5 ft. 10 in. in total length when complete, have covered one of the above-mentioued rock-graves. Gregorio's practised eye, and even my own, could see that the slopes to the south and west of the site were full of tombs, of which a very few only had been opened, and a large

[1] Mission en Phénicie, p. 288.

field presents itself for the energies of the *τυμβωρύχος*, if he succeed in making terms with the owners of the land—a syndicate of worthies described to me as the most *σκληροί* of all the hard-fisted Akanthiotes.

*Liches.* A little site called Liches, a mile and a-half to the west below the village of Kalorgá, where the peasants say that they have found *κεφάλια* and *ποδάρια*, and where we did in fact pick up some fragments, remains to be mentioned. The statuettes show similar bands of colour to the Kako-scale specimens mentioned above, and one held a bunch of grapes (?) in the left hand, as did two of the rough figures found at Amargetti.

So far we have traversed the least-known part of Cyprus; but on emerging from the rugged mountain-tract which lies west of Macaria, we join the beaten track of travellers, who, having skirted the southern slopes of the mountains, now cross the passes and descend into the broad and fertile strip extending from Agios Epiktetos to Cormachiti, which was in ancient times, as in modern, the richest and most civilised district in the island; and in the presence of macadamised roads, glazed windows, and Frank garments the occupation of the archaeological explorer is gone.

# CHAPTER III.

## MISCELLANEA.

THE antiquities of the central districts of Cyprus are too well known to need minute enumeration; a score of travellers have described Idalium, Chytri, Citium, Amathus, Tamassus, Curium, Nicosia, Famagusta, Kyrenïa, and all the lesser centres of classical and mediaeval interest in the Mesaoreá and the northern and southern hilly belts; and I propose only to collect in this concluding chapter a few disjecta membra from these districts which have escaped notice or been but recently discovered. I cannot claim so intimate a knowledge of the centre as of the extremities of the island, but have from time to time ridden hither and thither about it, either while staying in Nicosia or Larnaca, or in passing to or from Papho and the Carpass.

No point in Cyprian topography is more uncertain than the situation of Marium, the city whose inhabitants Ptolemy Lagus is said to have transferred to Paphos. Opinions have varied as to whether it should be looked for near the modern *Mari*, midway between Citium and Amathus, or whether it is not the earlier name of the Arsinoe whose remains lie under Poli-tis-Chrysochou, on the north coast of the island. The former view is held by (among others) Sakellarios (i. p. 57), Engel (i. p. 109), and M. Six (Revue Numismatique, 1883, p. 254), if we may judge by the apparently geographical order in which the latter ranges his autonomous cities of Cyprus. The latter view is however more frequently received, and has certainly much in its favour; Stephen of Byzantium directly asserts (s. v. *Μάριον*) that the name of Marium was changed to Arsinoe (but does not further particularize which town of that name is intended); even without the express statement of Diodorus (xix. 79) that the Marians were transferred to Paphos after the rebellion of their

*Marium.*

King Stasioecus, we might still infer that the name had ceased to exist in the Roman period from the fact that neither Strabo nor Ptolemy makes mention of it. The discoveries at Arsinoe in 1887 proved that a city much older than the Ptolemaic period had existed there, and the extraordinary amount of Attic pottery in its tombs—far in excess of all the examples of such ware previously found in Cyprus—recalls the statement in the Periplus of Scylax (s. v. *Κύπρος*), *Μάριον* Ἑλληνίς[1]. Further, it is easier to believe that the Marians were transported from Poli to the nearest city, New Paphos, a distance of only 25 miles, than from Mari for over 60 miles past Amathus and Curium and Old Paphos, to say nothing of smaller towns like Treta. In short, much goes to prove that, after Marium had been depopulated, it was refounded as Arsinoe, and perhaps this season's excavations will finally settle the point.

On the other side, there is very little literary evidence worth regarding: the mention of Marium by so late a writer as Pliny (N. H. v. 31) might be set against the silence of Strabo; and if the *Μάλος* which Cimon besieged[2] be really *Μάριον*, as seems certain, the probability of its being near Citium may be accounted of equal weight with the argument used above to show that it lay near New Paphos. But there would still remain the express statement of Stephen of Byzantium, and the necessity of finding an earlier name for Arsinoe. But nevertheless the persistence of an ancient name is not to be lightly disregarded, and my reason for bringing up this subject of Marium again is to place on record that remains do exist in the neighbourhood of *Mari* and *Maroni* of a town, whose tombs contain objects ranging from a very early to a very late period—in fact, quite compatible with an old and a newer foundation.

My attention was first directed to the neighbourhood by Mr. Cobham, Commissioner of Larnaca, who told me that reports had reached him of continual finds by the villagers of Maroni and Psemmatisméno, and acting on this I made a journey thither in the middle of August. I visited first Maroni, and found the villagers, as I had expected, extremely reticent; but promises, bribes, and assurances that I was no detective, so far opened

[1] It should be noticed that Scylax's (?) imperfect list apparently enumerates the cities in geographical order from Salamis round the north of the island to Amanthus, and, if this be so, the position of Marium between Soli and the latter is a strong argument in favour of Poli.

[2] Diod. Sic. xii. 3.

their hearts that I was conducted to a series of graves freshly opened in a hillside south of the village and looking towards the sea. The fragments of Graeco-Roman glass scattered about their mouths sufficiently indicated their character, and near them and subsequently in the village I found four inscribed cippi, whose lettering was of a very late period: like most of their class in Cyprus, these inscriptions are badly cut and spelt.

23. In the village :—

| ΟΛΥΜΠΙΑC | *'Ολυμπιὰς* |
|---|---|
| ΑΦΡΟΔΑΤΟCΓΥΝΗΧΡΗ | *'Αφροδᾶτος γυνὴ χρη-* |
| CΤΗΧΑΙΡΑΙ | *στὴ χαῖρ(ε).* |

For the name *'Αφροδᾶς* see Pape s. v.

24. Near the graves :—

| ΤΡΥΦΑΙ///ΙΑ | *Τρύφαι(ν)α* |
|---|---|
| ΑΡΙCΗΤΟC | *'Αριστῆτος* |
| Χ ΗCΤΗΧΑΙΡЄΝ | *χ[ρ]ηστὴ χαίρε(ι)ν.* |

25. Ibid. :—

| MARKIA | *Μαρκία* |
|---|---|
| MAPIV'' | *Μαρί(νου)* ? |
| XPHCTH | *χρηστὴ* |
| XΛ///////// | *χα[ῖρε.* |

26. Ibid., a mere scratch :—

? CΙΛCΙΧΡΗCΤΗ

On returning to the village I found that my character had been cleared of suspicion, and I was shown a private hoard of pottery which must have come from quite other graves than those which I had just visited, for it was of the true 'Paraskeve' type, i. e. unglazed ware, buff ground with hatchings in black or red, very thin, and rude in design; and this, I was informed, had been found nearer to the sea. I was further shown a Phoenician cylinder, but the jealous owner would neither permit a near inspection nor sell his treasure. I then tried Psemmatisméno, and found there red glazed ware with incised patterns of cross-hatching and wavy lines, also a 'Paraskeve' type: and next morning was conducted to the graves where the Maróni pottery had been found, all comparatively freshly opened in several localities in the charub-groves which stretch down to the sea. Corresponding to the large necropolis which had evidently been tapped only in haste and fear, I felt sure that there must be a city-site, and at last, after many questions, elicited from my guide the information that there was a place in the grove where big *τετράγωνες πέτρες* were always to be found when any native of Maróni wished to build himself a house. To this spot he conducted me, and we emerged at last upon a tract of undulating mounds from which peeped here and there the corners of squared blocks, one as much as 5 ft. × 2½: a second had a chisel-draft round the edges, as in the second period of old work at Kuklia; and I further picked up one of the convex stones with flat under-side which were found in numbers at Leontari Vouno, and which are supposed to indicate an early site; I have already mentioned their existence in the Carpass. Buried under the hillocks and arable land, appeared to lie remains of a town to which the graves around, both early and late, belong. General di Cesnola is said to have found Phoenician pottery in a knoll overlooking the sea, south of the site, but not to have seen the site itself; and Sakellarios rested his conjecture that the site of Marium was in this vicinity on a ruined church nearly a mile away. The site is near Maróni, but nearly three miles from Mari, where are no ancient remains whatever; and it is with much diffidence that I suggest that Marium, and later an Arsinoe, stood here, and that the earlier name has survived in those of the two villages.

*Tokhni.* Hardly a mile from Mari is a village, which enjoys a certain sanctity in Cyprus: this is Tokhni, where the Empress Helena, who had landed on her return from Jerusalem on the coast near Mari, made a bridge and founded the present church thereon. In this she left a fragment of the True Cross, and proceeded, so says Cypriote tradition, to hurl the 'devils' into a well which lies immediately north of the shrine. On a scarped rock above this well is cut in deep letters, coloured red, the following inscription:—

+ I Γ ⊓ ʒ Σ V I ⊬ I ⊬ ⊧

but what it signifies, in what alphabet it is expressed, whether it is a date or a magical formula or what else in the world, no one who has copied it has been able to determine.

The Commissioner (Mr. C. D. Cobham) has a fragment of a pedestal, which was found in a wall at Old Larnaca a short time ago. I publish it with his permission. The lettering is late, and the stone is broken right and top? *Larnaca.*

28.

Α Ρ Χ Ι Ε Ρ Ε Α Τ Η Σ Ρ Ω
Τ Ο Ν Α Γ Ω Ν Ο Θ Ε Τ Η
Π Ε Ν Τ Α Ε Τ Η Ρ Ι Δ Ι Κ Α
Τ Ο Η L Ε Φ Ο Υ Π Ρ Ϲ
¯ Ο Α Λ Ι Μ Μ Α Ε Τ Ε Ϲ

[Ἡ πόλις ἡ Κιτιέων]
[τὸν δεῖνα τοῦ δεῖνος]
ἀρχιερέα τῆς Ῥώ[μης
τὸν ἀγωνοθέτη[ν τῇ
πενταετηρίδι κα[τὰ
τὸ ἡ L· ἐφ' οὗ πρῶ[τον
τὸ ἄλ(ε)ιμμα ἐτέθ[η.

The base of a statue of a high priest of the local worship of the Genius of Rome[1], and president for a period of five years of the games held in connection with the cult, such period being the eighth since the games were instituted (?). In his term the supplying of oil to the competitors gratis was instituted. The explanation given above of the words τῇ πενταετηρίδι κατὰ τὸ ἡ L appears to me to be the only one possible. The sign L in Cyprus usually means 'year'; but in this case that seems to be

[1] I ought to state that Mr. E. A. Gardner, who copied this stone previously to myself, read ΡΟ at the end of line 1, and thence restored ΡΟ[ΔΟΥ; but, besides my conviction that I was not mistaken as to the Ω, the title ἀρχιερεὺς τῆς Ῥόδου would be passing strange, and the Paphos inscription (J. H. S. ix. p. 254), by which it might be supported, is too fragmentary to be relied upon.

precluded both by the words *κατὰ τὸ ἡ* L not coming between *πενταετηρίδι* and its article, and by the use of *κατά*.

The following late cippi I copied at the site of *Tremithus* (Tremithoussa in the Mesaoréa):—

29. ΟΝΑϹΙΧΡΗϹΤΕ *Ὀνάσι χρηστέ.*

The existence of the name *Ὀνάσις*, though not hitherto found, cannot be questioned as the forms *Ὀνασᾶς* (*supr.* p. 24) and *Ὀνασίον* (Pape) are known in Cyprus, cf. also the frequent *Ὀνασίκυπρος* (e.g. *supr.* p. 89).

30. ΣΥΜΜΑΧΕ *Σύμμαχε*
ΧΡΗϹΤΕ *χρηστὲ*
ΧΑΙΡΕ *χαῖρε.*

31. ЄΠΑΦΡΟ/ *Ἐπαφρό[διτε*
ΧΡΗϹΤ// *χρηστ[ὲ*
ΧЄΡЄ *χερε.*

32. ΤΙ *Τι[μόθεε?*
ΧΡΗϹ Ε *χρησ[τ]ὲ*
ΧΕΡΕ *χερε.*

*Kuklia (Mesaoréa).* When riding from Athieno to Famagusta I happened to stop for a few hours at the village of Kuklia in the Mesaoréa, and was informed by the cafeji of the existence of a written stone in the Turkish graveyard. It proved to be a limestone pedestal much chipped, a large hole having been made in the surface at the right bottom corner, but it was otherwise complete. The lettering was late, and somewhat irregularly distributed, the upper lines not filling the stone up to the end.

33. ΤΟΚΟΙΝΟΝ ΚΥΠΡΙΩΝ
ΚΕΙΩΝΙΑΝΚΑΛΛΙΣΤΩΑΤΤΙΚΗΝ
Γ////ΝΑΙΚΑΦΛΑΥΙΟΥΙ///////////////ΙΕ//////
//////////ΘΕΝΟΥΝω Ϲ//////////////////////
//////////ΓΑΘΟΥ Χ////////

Τὸ κοινὸν Κυπρίων
Κειωνίαν Καλλιστὼ Ἀττικὴν
γ[υ]ναῖκα Φλαυίου Ἰ[ουλιανοῦ ?] ἱέ[ρειαν
τῆς Παρ]θένου . . . . . . . . . . . . .
. . . ἀ]γαθοῦ . . . . .

It seems impossible to make more of this. Ἀττικήν must be a name in spite of the unusual number of appellatives with which this lady is endowed already.

If the restoration of line 4, given above, is correct, the Παρθένος occurs here for the first time in Cyprus. As Prof. W. M. Ramsay has pointed out to me, this *avatar* of the Asiatic Goddess, 'the unwedded mother of all life,' is known already at Perga of Pamphylia on the shores opposite Cyprus; and thence he has traced her northwards to Ephesus and to the Maeander Valley, as Artemis or Artemis-Leto (see a forthcoming article on Artemis-Leto and Apollo Lairbenos in J. H. S. vol. x). M. Reinach (Revue des études grecques i. 1, p. 36) collects instances of her presence at Halicarnassus and in the north. How easily such a cult might be assimilated in late times with that of the Asiatic Aphrodite in Cyprus it is needless to emphasize.

It is worthy of note, however, that the Mesaoréan Kuklia lies about midway between two great Cyprian religious centres where the name of the Ϝάνασσα or Aphrodite has not been found, at least in inscriptions: these are Salamis and (strange to say) Idalium, whereas in both the chief goddess is *Athena*. The Salaminian temple of Athena Pronoea has been already mentioned (p. 62), and in nearly all the Cypriote inscriptions of Dali, Athena appears as the great goddess. Yet the unanimous testimony of ancient authors makes Idalium a favored seat of Aphrodite, and the conclusion seems inevitable that the Great Goddess of Cyprus, known in early times (vide Cypriote inscriptions passim) *not* as Aphrodite, but as ἡ Ϝάνασσα or ἡ Παφίja, was confounded by the western Greeks and Anatolians with not one, but several, of their goddesses who happened to possess one or more of her attributes. The poets established a tradition in favour of Aphrodite, but to Anatolians she appeared to be their Παρθένος, and possibly Greek settlers from the west noticed her predominant celibate character, and identified her with their virgin-goddess Athena. It is possible of course that the Idalian Athena is a deity of distinct origin, imported or evolved by the native Cyprians, but it should be remarked that the Cypriote texts of Dali, in which her name occurs, are among the later examples of the script, and if she is posterior in time to the *Ϝάνασσα*, she was probably confounded with her.

In any case, it is probable that the *Παρθένος* of whom Ceionia Callisto Atticé was priestess, was not very clearly distinguished either from the *Ϝάνασσα* who was supreme in the west and north of Cyprus, or from Athena who ruled over the south and east.

*Roman milestone.* In a field between Agios Epiktetos and Bellapaix I was shown a Roman milestone, whose hopeless condition accounts for its never having been published. Besides the intentional erasure of a whole line, centuries of wear and of use as a turning-post for the plough have obliterated almost every letter, and I could read only these disjointed scraps:—

| | | |
|---|---|---|
| 34. | . . . . . . . . . . . | . . . . . . . . . . . |
| | . . . . . . . . . . . | . . . . . . . . . . . |
| | erasure | . . . . . . . . . . . |
| | Λ U C . . . . . | Aug(ustum) |
| | . . . . . . . . . . . | . . . . . . . . . . . |
| | . . C Є B | . . Σεβ[αστὸν . . |
| | . . Ρ Χ Ι Ε Ρ Ε / | ἀ]ρχιερέ(α) [μέγιστον |
| | Λ Ε | λε΄. |

The last line appeared to be complete, and therefore this is in all probability the 35th milestone on the road from Salamis to Lapethus. As the crow flies, the spot where it stands is distant just under 29 English miles from the former, which leaves a reasonable margin for the windings of the road and the slight excess of the English over the Roman mile.

*Lapethus.* At Lapethus I found nothing new, and I convinced myself that excavation there would never repay a large outlay. The only objects of real interest on the later site are the rock-cut sea-baths—oblong basins into which the waves flow and ebb again by means of supply- and waste-channels: the harbour is a mere angle of the coast open on two sides; and the character of the débris is most unpromising. Of the older town which stood on the site of modern Lapithos, and on the hills above, no trace remains but a few tombs.

*Larnaca-tis-Lapithou.*

At Larnaca-tis-Lapithou I copied once more the pedestal erected by the priests of Poseidon to Numenius, son of Numenius[1], and assured myself beyond all possibility of doubt that the title given to Poseidon in line 6 is *τοῦ Ναρν[α]κίου*, *not* *Λαρν[α]κίου*, as it has been previously copied. I subsequently found that both Dr. Guillemard and Mr. Louis Dyer, who were in Cyprus in the course of 1888, had read a *Ν*, not a *Λ*. This dispels the pleasing illusion that Larnaca is an ancient name.

*Soli.*

The site of Soli is, I fear, no more worth exploration than that of Lapethus, and I saw no single spot wherein to dig with profit, unless it be on the edges of the marsh which marks the former harbour. The ancient buildings have been quarried to build Morphou and Lefka, or towns on the Karamanian coast. By the kindness of Mr. King, the Commissioner of Nicosia, I copied in his office an inscription found in the Solia valley and conveyed to the metropolis as a marketable commodity. It is a slab, broken right and bottom: the lettering is regular but late:—

| | | |
|---|---|---|
| 35. | ΑΥΤΟΚΡΑΤΟΡΑΚΑΙ | *Αὐτοκράτορα Καί[σαρα* |
| | Μ·ΑΥΡΗΛΙΟΝΑΝΤΩ | *Μ. Αὐρήλιον Ἀντω[νεῖ-* |
| | ΝΟΝϹЄΒΑϹΤΟΝ | *νον Σεβαστὸν [οἱ πά-* |
| | ΙΑΙΑΡΞΑΝΤЄϹΓ | *(λ)αι ? ἄρξαντες Π[το-* |
| | ΛЄΜΑΙΟϹ⌒Ν | *λεμαῖος Ὀν[ησάνδρου* |
| | ///////ΙϹ//// | *[καὶ ὁ δεῖνα τοῦ δεῖνος].* |

I cannot restore quite satisfactorily the letters preceding *ἄρξαντες*. Some association of past magistrates is referred to like *οἱ γεγυμνασιαρχηκότες* and *ἐστρατηγηκότες* of Old Paphos (J.H.S. ix. inscr. nos. 105, 3.) The preceding letters may belong to a compound of *-αρχω*.

I also copied once more and took impressions of the 'Sergius Paulus' inscription, now built into the threshold of a store in Karavastasi. The owner derives a small revenue from digging it out afresh, and showing it for a consideration to each passing archaeologist; and all my persuasion and threats availed not to deter him from replacing it in a position where every one passing through the door must tread on it. Already the upper line has been worn away since General di Cesnola copied it, and the whole will soon be hopelessly defaced.

[1] Published in Le Bas and Waddington, No. 2779: also in Cesnola, 'Cyprus,' p. 421.

I copied it again rather to verify the name Paulus, than with any view to republishing the whole inscription, but I find, on comparing my copy with that of General di Cesnola, some important variants from his readings, which, added to the fact that I have recovered some more letters in the right-hand half, make it worth while to reprint the text in full.

36. Marble block built into the threshold of Christodoulo's store at Karavastasi: lettering small but not very regular —very much worn at the right side and top:—

[ΑΠΟΛΛΩΝΙΟϹΤΩΠΑΤ] (This line, being now worn away, I take from Cesnola.)

ΚΑΙΤΗΜΗΤΡΙΑΡΙ . . . . . . . . . . . . . . . . . . . . .

ΤΟΝΠΕΡΙΒΟΛΟΝΚΑΙΤΗΝ . . . . . . . . . . . . . . . . ΙΑϹ

ΥΜΩΝΑΥΤΩΝΕΝΤΟΛΑϹϹΝ . . . . . . . . . . . ΙϹΤ . . .

ΕΑΥΤΟΥΤΗϹϹΟΛΙΩΝΠΟΛΕΩϹ . . . . . ΝΟ . . . . . .

ΠΑΡΧΗϹΑϹΓΡΑΝΜΑΤΕΥϹΑϹΑΡΧΙL . . . . . . . . . . . . . . .

ΒΥΒΛΙΟΦΥΛΑΚΙΟΥΓΕΝΟΜΕΝΟϹ LΙΓ . . . . . . . . . . . .

ΞΟΥϹΙΟΥ Κ̄Ε̄ ΤΙΜΗΤΕΥϹΑϹΤΗΝΒΟΥΛ . . . . .
ΛΕΞΑϹΤΩΝΕΠΙΠΑΥΛΟΥ . . . .

ΠΑΤΟΥ.

*'Απολλώνιος τῷ πατ[ρὶ τῷ δεῖνι τοῦ δεῖνος*
*καὶ τῇ μητρὶ 'Αρτ[εμιδώρᾳ τοῦ δεῖνος καθιερῶσε*
*τὸν περίβολον καὶ τὴν [στήλην? ταύτην κατὰ] τὰς*
*ὑμῶν αὐτῶν ἐντολὰς . . . . . . . . . . . . . . . .*
*ἑαυτοῦ τῆς Σολίων πόλεως, [ἀγορα]νο[μήσας, ἐ-*
*παρχήσας, γρα(μ)ματεύσας, ἀρχιε[ρασάμενος, ἐπὶ τοῦ*
*βυβλιοφυλακίου γενόμενος· Lιγ[. μηνὸς δημαρχε-*
*ξουσίου κέ. τιμητεύσας τὴν βουλ[ὴν δι-*
*(ὰ) ἐξ(ετ)αστῶν ἐπὶ Παύλου [ἀνθυ-*
*πάτου.*

The last two lines and a half after the date are proved, both by their matter and by the use of a different form of *xi*, to be later additions, inscribed afterwards to complete the list of Apollonius' offices. I conceive them to refer to some special reconstitution of the senate of Soli in the time of the proconsul Paulus, Apollonius having been commissioned to revise the list in the capacity of censor (τιμητεύω)[1]. It will be noticed, if my reading is compared with that in Cesnola, that I have eliminated the '*Παμμάτειρα*' in line 6. I subjoin a translation:—

'Apollonius to his father .... son of .... and to his mother Artemidora daughter of ... consecrated the enclosure and this monument according to your own (i.e. his parents') commands ...... having filled the offices of clerk of the market, prefect, town-clerk, high priest, and having been in charge of the record-office. Erected on the 25th of the month Demarchexusius in the year . 13. He also revised the senate by means of assessors in the time of the proconsul Paulus.'

The great interest of this inscription lies in the possible allusion to the Sergius Paulus of Acts xiii. There can be no good reason for doubting an identification, which would unquestionably have been proposed and hardly disputed had Sergius Paulus been known from any other source than the New Testament. The lettering is quite that of the first century. It is much to be regretted that the third and most important letter in the date of the year is hopelessly lost: if it was, as I believe, Ρ, then, reckoning from the establishment of the province, we get A.D. 55 for the date of this inscription. St. Paul's visit fell in 45, and it is evident from the wording of the last lines that Paulus had ceased to hold office for some time previous to the erection of this monument. Without being at all desirous to find correspondances with Holy Writ still existing all over the East, few can refuse to identify a 'Paulus proconsul' with the only known governor of that name who held office in Cyprus[2]. Whatever opinion be held about this identification, the stone ought to be rescued from its present precarious position, and lodged in safety: it would be an interesting addition to the Government collection now in process of formation at Nicosia.

[1] The reading διὰ ἐξ(ετ)αστῶν as well as minor points in the interpretation were suggested by Prof. W. M. Ramsay.

[2] Böckh erroneously supposed Paullus Fabius Maximus to have been proconsul of Cyprus; but M. Waddington has shown this to be a mistake: see the Appendix to this volume.

# APPENDIX.

## PROCONSULAR GOVERNORS OF CYPRUS.

It may be useful to state, however imperfectly, how the list of Proconsular Governors stands at the present date, and how far the enumeration made by Engel (vol. i. pp. 459 foll.), and later by Marquardt (Röm. Staatsv. i. p. 391), can be supplemented or corrected. Had M. Waddington's Fasti of the provinces of Cilicia and Cyprus been published, the task would have been superfluous.

When Cyprus was first incorporated with the province of Cilicia (i.e. in 55 B.C.) under the rule of P. Cornelius Lentulus Spinther, a special quaestor, C. Sextius Rufus, was detached to look after its interests; but the names of his successors under subsequent proconsuls of Cilicia we do not know, although it is probable that the Quintus Volusius, sent to the island by Marcus Cicero in 51 B.C., 'ne cives Romani pauci qui illic negotiantur jus sibi dictum negarent' (ad Att. v. 21), held the office in question. However, before four years had elapsed, Caesar bestowed Cyprus on Arsinoe and Ptolemy, and eleven years later it passed by Antony's gift to the children of Cleopatra. Meanwhile we hear in 39 B.C. of a certain Demetrius, a freedman of Julius Caesar's, being sent by Antony to look after the island (Dio Cass. 48. 40). It was not until 27 B.C. that it was resumed as an imperial province, and five years later Augustus exchanged it (together with Gallia Narbonensis) for Dalmatia with the Senate, and from henceforward it was governed by propraetors with the 'brevet' rank of proconsul, under whom were a legatus and quaestor. Of these governors we know about twenty names in the next two centuries from ancient authors, inscriptions, and coins, and I enumerate them approximately in order of date.

(Augustus) *Aulus Plautius* known from a coin (Head, Hist. Num. p 627).

*P. Paquius Scaeva*, stated in an inscription of Histonium (C. I. L. ix. 2845) to have been sent 'extra sortem' for the second time in the reign of Caligula 'ad componendum statum in reliquum provinciae Cypri.' He had therefore formerly been proconsul, and Marquardt fixes his term in the reign of Augustus.

(Tiberius) *Quintus?* . . . *Telesinus?* grandson of Q. Hortensius, the orator, probably through his daughter, Hortensia. The prenomen and cognomen are restored conjecturally from a broken palimpsest inscription of Old Paphos, published imperfectly in J. H. S. ix. p. 251: for the gentile name there appears to be no evidence, as the name of Hortensia's husband has not been recorded, so far as I can discover. Thus nothing is assured except the fact that a grandson of the orator governed Cyprus in the reign of Tiberius. The unusual mention of the *maternal* grandfather is explained by his fame.

*Lucius Axius Naso*, known from an inscription of Lapethus (Le Bas and Wadd. 2773). His exact date is recorded—29 A.D.—and the names of his legatus and quaestor, M. Etrilius Lupercus and C. Flavius Figulus.

*C. Ummidius Durmius Quadratus*, known from an inscription of Casinum (C. I. L. x. 5182). Liebenam (Forsch. z. Verwaltungs Gesch. d. Römischen Kaiserreichs, p. 157) places his term in Cyprus in the reign of Tiberius. He is identical with G. Ummidius Quadratus, high-priest of Paphos, honoured in an inscription (Le Bas and Wadd. 2801), now built into the church wall at Kuklia. Cp. also an inscription found by us in the Temple, and published J. H. S. ix. p. 237, No. 41.

(Claudius) *T. Cominius Proculus*, known only from a coin quoted in Cohen, i. 262, No. 132.

*Sergius Paulus*, proconsul during St. Paul's visit in 45 A.D. (Acts xiii. 7).

*Quintus Julius Cordus*, recorded in an inscription of Citium (C. I. G. 2631). He was proconsul in 51 A.D.

*L. Annius Bassus* succeeded the above (inscr. of Curium C. I. G. 2632).

(Before Nero) ? *L. Laberius Cocceius Lepidus* (C. I. L. vi. 1440; cf. Borghesi, v. 251) is mentioned in a Roman inscription simply as proconsul, province not named, but the dedicator is one 'Apollonius limenarcha Cypri.' Borghesi dates him before Nero.

| | | |
|---|---|---|
| ? 1st century. | *Varius Rufus* | known from undated inscriptions of Old Paphos (J. H. S. ix. Nos. 49, 68, 104, 114), but, as no Emperor's name was found there later than Domitian, I have ascribed these proconsuls conjecturally to the 1st century. |
| ? Do. | *Lucius Coelius Tarphinus ?* | |
| ? Do | *D. Plautius Felix Iulianus* | |
| ? Do. | *Lucius Vilius Maronius* | names found in an inscription of New Paphos, published supr. p. 8, and in one published by Le Bas and Wadd. 2814. The lettering of both appears to be not later than the 1st century. |
| ? Do. | *Quintus Caelius Honoratus* | |
| (Trajan) | ..... *Flaccus*, known from a fragmentary inscription of Salamis (C. I. G. 2638). | |
| (Hadrian) | *Ti. Claudius Juncus* (inscription of Citium, Le Bas and Wadd. 2726). According to M. Waddington he was a consul suffectus in 127 A.D. | |
| (Severus) | *Audius Bassus* recorded on a milestone of 198 A.D. (Le Bas and Wadd. 2806). | |
| | *Sextus Clodius . . . (I)ulianus ?* (inscription of Citium, Le Bas and Wadd. 2728) | |
| (Elagabalus) | *Claudius Attalus.* (Dio Cass. 79. 3.) | |

To what reign *L. Gabo Arunculeius Pacilius Severus*, styled proconsul designate of Cyprus in an inscription of Brixia (C. I. L. v. 4332), is to be assigned there is no evidence to show.

As Liebenam (p. 120) definitely accepts Waddington's emendation of Κυ(ρήνης) for Κύπρου in C. I. G. 3548, we must strike the name of *C. Antius Aulus Julius Quadratus* from the list of Cyprian governors; but it is to be noted that no one has read anything but Κύπρου on the stone itself, and it is not quite impossible that Quadratus obtained the two provinces successively, though Böckh's theory of the combination of the provinces under the same proconsul is untenable. Marquardt, however, omits the name, and it is best to follow him until the stone (if still in existence) be re-examined.

I have also omitted the name of *Paullus Fabius Maximus*, supposed by Böckh (on C. I. G. 2629), by Engel, and by Marquardt, to have been proconsul of Cyprus after his consulship in 11 B.C. (Mon. Ancyr. i. 38, etc.). As M. Waddington points out (Fastes, No. 59), the Paphian inscription in honour of his wife Marcia, which does *not* add ἀνθύπατος after the husband's name, really affords presumption that he *never* governed Cyprus,—and there is no other evidence on the point.

*L. Flavius Septimius Aper Octavianus* (Engel, p. 462, C. I. L. vi. 1415) was quaestor in the island, and besides him and the two under L. Axius Naso, recorded above, the following magistrates are known :—

(Before Vespasian?) *L. Servenius Cornutus*, quaestor (inscr. of Acmonia in Phrygia, published by W. M. Ramsay in Amer. Journ. of Arch. 1885, p. 148).

(Nerva) *L. Julius Marinus Caecilius Simplex*, legatus (inscr. of Cures Sabini, C. I. L. ix. 4965).

(Hadrian) *M. Calpurnius Rufus*, legatus (inscr. of Ephesus, C. I. L. iii. 6072).

*L. Aquillius Florus Turcianus Gallus*, proquaestor (inscr. of Athens, C. I. L. iii. 551).

? *M. Campanius Marcellus*, procurator Augusti (inscr. of Capua, C. I. L. x. 3847).

? *T. Flavius Philinus*, legatus (inscr. of Thespiae, Rhein. Mus. 1843, p. 105).

Certain other inscriptions (C. I. L. vi. 1651; x. 525, 3761, 7351) refer to magistrates of Cyprus, but the names are lost. It is to be expected that the forthcoming excavations on the site of Salamis will fill up several gaps in the proconsular *fasti* of the island.

# INDEX.

THE END.

www.ingramcontent.com/pod-product-compliance
Ingram Content Group UK Ltd.
Pitfield, Milton Keynes, MK11 3LW, UK
UKHW042156280225
455719UK00001B/365

9 781108 041935